Addition of Time

Name _____

60 seconds	= 1 minute (min)	7 days	= 1 week (wk)
60 minutes	= 1 hour (h)	4 weeks	= 1 month (mo)
24 hours	= 1 day (d)	12 months or 52 weeks	= 1 year (y)

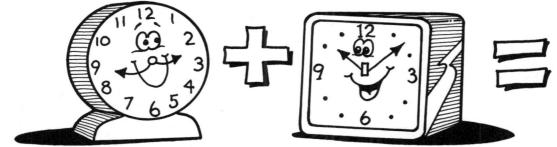

Complete.

1.
```
    2 h    14 min
+   3 h    31 min
```

2.
```
    5 h    24 min
+   7 h    19 min
```

3.
```
    3 min  14 s
+   4 min  18 s
```

4.
```
    5 min  41 s
+   3 min  29 s
```

5.
```
    3 h    43 min
+   2 h    51 min
```

6.
```
    3 h    14 min
+   6 h    72 min
```

7.
```
    2 min  18 s
+   7 min  58 s
```

8.
```
    9 h    30 min
+   3 h    31 min
```

9.
```
    1 min  49 s
+   2 min  27 s
```

10.
```
    3 h    41 min
+   4 h    59 min
```

11.
```
    8 min  29 s
+   3 min  46 s
```

12.
```
    2 h    39 min
+   5 h    41 min
```

13.
```
    5 wk   2 d
+   2 wk   4 d
```

14.
```
    3 h    16 min
+   1 h    48 min
```

15.
```
    2 d    4 h
+   3 d    15 h
```

16.
```
    3 d    15 h
+   4 d    10 h
```

17.
```
    6 wk   3 d
+   1 wk   9 d
```

18.
```
    16 h   51 min
+   4 h    8 min
```

19.
```
    5 min  27 s
+   14 min 33 s
```

20.
```
    3 y    8 mo
+   2 y    6 mo
```

IF8747 Math Topics

Subtraction of Time

Name _____

60	seconds	=	1 minute (min)	7	days	=	1 week (wk)
60	minutes	=	1 hour (h)	4	weeks	=	1 month (mo)
24	hours	=	1 day (d)	12	months or 52 weeks	=	1 year (y)

Complete.

1.
```
    7  min  42 s
 -  3  min  29 s
_____
```

2.
```
    5  h      49 min
 -  2  h      34 min
_____
```

3.
```
    8  h      24 min
 -  5  h      19 min
_____
```

4.
```
    4  min  47 s
 -  3  min  28 s
_____
```

5.
```
    8  h      14 min
 -  3  h      25 min
_____
```

6.
```
    7  h      29 min
 -  2  h      38 min
_____
```

7.
```
    9  min  23 s
 -  8  min  51 s
_____
```

8.
```
    4  min  21 s
 -  2  min  53 s
_____
```

9.
```
   12 min  19 s
 -  8 min  42 s
_____
```

10.
```
    5  h      14 min
 -  3  h      29 min
_____
```

11.
```
   16 min  42 s
 -  8 min  25 s
_____
```

12.
```
    3  h      12 min
 -  1  h      46 min
_____
```

13.
```
    5  d    9  h
 -  2  d   10  h
_____
```

14.
```
    3  wk   4  d
 -  1  wk   5  d
_____
```

15.
```
   16  d   14  h
 -  9  d    7  h
_____
```

16.
```
    6  y    4  mo
 -  3  y    6  mo
_____
```

17.
```
    5  min  21 s
 -  2  min  22 s
_____
```

18.
```
    8  d    7  h
 -  5  d   21  h
_____
```

19.
```
    5  wk   3  d
 -  2  wk   6  d
_____
```

20.
```
   13  h    14 min
 -  7  h    48 min
_____
```

21.
```
    8  y    9  mo
 -  2  y   10  mo
_____
```

22.
```
    4  d   13  h
 -  1  d   17  h
_____
```

23.
```
   21  h    10 min
 -  8  h    54 min
_____
```

24.
```
    4  min  32 s
 -  2  min  47 s
_____
```

IF8747 Math Topics

Different Ways of Telling Time

Complete.

Name _____

_____ minutes after _____

_____ minutes before _____

_____ minutes after _____

_____ minutes before _____

_____ minutes after _____

_____ minutes before _____

_____ minutes after _____

_____ minutes before _____

_____ minutes after _____

_____ minutes before _____

_____ minutes after _____

_____ minutes before _____

_____ minutes after _____

_____ minutes before _____

_____ minutes after _____

_____ minutes before _____

_____ minutes after _____

_____ minutes before _____

_____ minutes after _____

_____ minutes before _____

_____ minutes after _____

_____ minutes before _____

Time Conversion – I

Name _____

60 seconds	= 1 minute (min)	7 days	= 1 week (wk)
60 minutes	= 1 hour (h)	4 weeks	= 1 month (mo)
24 hours	= 1 day (d)	12 months or 52 weeks	= 1 year (y)

Complete.

1. 3 h = _____ min

2. 4 d = _____ h

3. 2 h = _____ min

4. 5 min = _____ s

5. 6 min = _____ s

6. 8 h = _____ min

7. 2 d = _____ h

8. 5 h = _____ min

9. 5 d = _____ h

10. 14 min = _____ s

11. 240 min = _____ h

12. 7 d = _____ h

13. 96 h = _____ d

14. 300 s = _____ min

15. 8 min = _____ s

16. $\frac{1}{6}$ d = _____ h

17. 9 h = _____ min

18. 180 min = _____ h

19. $\frac{1}{3}$ min = _____ s

20. 3 d = _____ h

21. 12 h = _____ min

22. 8 d = _____ h

23. 120 h = _____ d

24. 540 s = _____ min

Time Conversion – II

Name _____

60 seconds	= 1 minute (min)	7 days	= 1 week (wk)
60 minutes	= 1 hour (h)	4 weeks	= 1 month (mo)
24 hours	= 1 day (d)	12 months or 52 weeks	= 1 year (y)

Complete.

1.
   50 h = ____ d ____ h

2.
   72 s = ____ min ____ s

3.
   12 min 12s = ____ s

4.
   9 d = ____ wk ____ d

5.
   2 d 6 hr = ____ h

6.
   26 h = ____ d ____ h

7.
   129s = ____ min ____ s

8.
   37 d = ____ wk ____ d

9.
   189 min = ____ h ____ min

10.
   4 d 4 hr = ____ h

11.
   53 d = ____ wk ____ d

12.
   78 h = ____ d ____ h

13.
   5 min 14 s = ____ s

14.
   484 min = ____ h ____ min

15.
   6 wk 2 d = ____ d

16.
   65 d = ____ wk ____ d

17.
   369 s = ____ min ____ s

18.
   2 wk 6 d = ____ d

19.
   3 mo 2 wk = ____ wk

20.
   55 wk = ____ y ____ wk

21.
   16 mo = ____ y ____ mo

22.
   88 d = ____ wk ____ d

23.
   50 d = ____ wk ____ d

24.
   39 wk = ____ mo ____ wk

Elapsed Time – I

Name _____

How much time has gone by?

1. **From**   **To**

P.M.   P.M.

_____ minutes

2. **From**   **To**

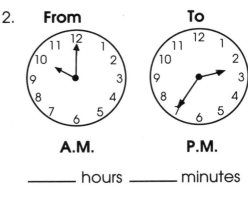

A.M.   P.M.

_____ hours _____ minutes

3. **From**   **To**

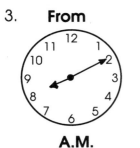

A.M.   P.M.

_____ hours _____ minutes

4. **From**   **To**

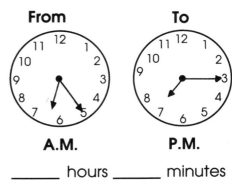

A.M.   P.M.

_____ hours _____ minutes

5. **From**   **To**

A.M.   P.M.

_____ hours _____ minutes

6. **From**   **To**

P.M.   A.M.

_____ hours _____ minutes

7. **From**   **To**

A.M.   P.M.

_____ hours _____ minutes

8. **From**   **To**

P.M.   A.M.

_____ hours _____ minutes

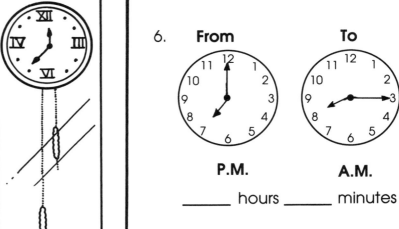

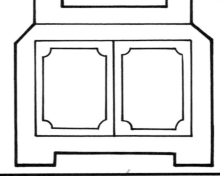

IF8747 Math Topics

Elapsed Time – II

Name _____

How much time has gone by?

1.

From	To
9:05	3:10
A.M.	P.M.

_____ h _____ min

2.

From	To
6:15	12:25
A.M.	P.M.

_____ h _____ min

3.

From	To
6:15	7:00
A.M.	P.M.

_____ h _____ min

4.

From	To
4:50	6:10
P.M.	P.M.

_____ h _____ min

5.

From	To
4:25	5:41
P.M.	P.M.

_____ h _____ min

6.

From	To
7:50	9:10
A.M.	A.M.

_____ h _____ min

7.

From	To
9:25	8:00
A.M.	P.M.

_____ h _____ min

8.

From	To
5:05	9:15
P.M.	P.M.

_____ h _____ min

9.

From	To
12:00	1:00
A.M.	P.M.

_____ h _____ min

10.

From	To
6:00	3:00
A.M.	P.M.

_____ h _____ min

Addition of Elapsed Time

Name _____

Figure the elapsed time.

1.

+ 50 minutes

Time: _____

2.

+ 1 hour 5 minutes

Time: _____

3.

+ 2 hours 40 minutes

Time: _____

4.

+ 25 minutes

Time: _____

5.

+ 30 minutes

Time: _____

6.

+ 4 hours 35 minutes

Time: _____

7.

+ 2 hours 20 minutes

Time: _____

8.

+ 4 hours

Time: _____

9.

+ 3 hours 15 minutes

Time: _____

10.

+ 20 minutes

Time: _____

11.

+ 6 hours 30 minutes

Time: _____

12.

+ 3 hours 30 minutes

Time: _____

13.

+11 hours

Time: _____

14.

+ 24 hours 5 minutes

Time: _____

More Addition of Time

Name _____

Determine the sum total.

A. Geneva worked on her sculpture this week:

Monday:	2 h	14 min
Tuesday:		30 min
Wednesday:	1 h	16 min
Thursday:	3 h	25 min
Friday:	1 h	45 min

Sum total: _____ _____

B. Monica's choir practice this week:

Monday:		55 min
Tuesday:		45 min
Wednesday:		30 min
Thursday:		50 min
Friday:	1 h	20 min

Sum total: _____ _____

C. David's swim practice this week:

Monday:	1 h	25 min
Tuesday:		43 min
Wednesday:	1 h	59 min
Thursday:	3 h	29 min
Friday:	1 h	37 min

Sum total: _____ _____

D. Eva's rollerblade club met for five Saturdays in a row:

Saturday #1:	2 h	12 min
Saturday #2:	3 h	51 min
Saturday #3:	1 h	43 min
Saturday #4:	3 h	49 min
Saturday #5:	2 h	29 min

Sum total: _____ _____

E. Michele went horseback riding with her friends for five Saturdays in a row:

Saturday #1:	1 h	50 min
Saturday #2:	2 h	5 min
Saturday #3:	3 h	10 min
Saturday #4:	1 h	42 min
Saturday #5:	1 h	27 min

Sum total: _____ _____

F. Mark's model rocket club met and built rockets for 5 Saturdays in a row:

Saturday #1:	2 h	35 min
Saturday #2:	3 h	21 min
Saturday #3:	2 h	41 min
Saturday #4:	1 h	56 min
Saturday #5:	3 h	29 min

Sum total: _____ _____

More Elapsed Time

Name _____

Complete.

Time Now	Add this Elapsed Time	Future Time (Include Day and Time)
1. Monday, 9:00 a.m.	2 days, 4 hours	_____
2. Saturday, 4:00 p.m.	3 days, 5 hours, 32 minutes	_____
3. Tuesday, 6:00 a.m.	6 days, 7 hours, 45 minutes	_____
4. Sunday, 1:00 p.m.	1 day, 9 hours, 56 minutes	_____
5. Thursday, 2:45 p.m.	5 days, 2 hours, 45 minutes	_____
6. Wednesday, 4:00 a.m.	8 days, 12 hours, 29 minutes	_____
7. Monday, 7:00 a.m.	14 days, 7 hours, 39 minutes	_____
8. Friday, 7:00 p.m.	2 days, 3 advanced time zones	_____
9. Monday, 5:00 p.m.	4 days, 25 hours	_____
10. Saturday, 12:00 a.m.	6 days, 13 hours, 1 minute	_____
11. Tuesday, 5:00 p.m.	12 days, 14 hours, 23 minutes	_____
12. Sunday, 2:00 a.m.	3 days, 26 hours	_____
13. Monday, 1:00 p.m.	2 weeks, 4 days, 35 minutes	_____
14. Saturday, 6:00 a.m.	74 hours	_____
15. Sunday, 8:00 a.m.	21 days, 2 hours	_____
16. Wednesday, 4:00 a.m.	15 days, 12 hours, 45 minutes	_____
17. Friday, 3:00 p.m.	5 days, 3 hours, 128 minutes	_____
18. Thursday, 6:00 p.m.	3 days, 4 earlier time zones	_____

Complete. Give the elapsed time in days and hours.

1. Monday, 4:00 a.m. to Wednesday, 5:00 a.m.   _____

2. Wednesday, 12:00 p.m. to Saturday, 2:00 p.m.   _____

3. Friday, 5:00 a.m. to Sunday, 4:00 p.m.   _____

4. Thursday, 7:00 p.m. to Friday, 9:00 a.m.   _____

5. Saturday, 6:00 p.m. to Monday, 5:00 a.m.   _____

6. Tuesday, 3:00 p.m. to Friday, 6:00 p.m.   _____

7. Saturday, 8:00 p.m. to Sunday, 3:00 a.m.   _____

8. Monday, 4:00 p.m. to Wednesday, 8:00 a.m.   _____

Bar Graphs

Name _____

1. Which vegetable proved to be the most productive? _____

2. What is the range of harvested vegetables in this garden? _____

3. How many more ears of corn were picked than onions? _____

4. What was the average (or mean) number of vegetables picked this season? _____

Rocketflash Elementary's School Garden

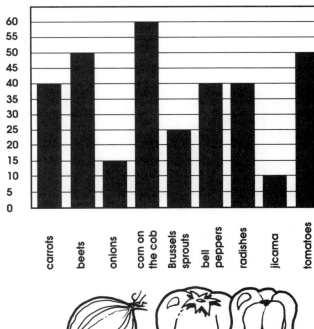

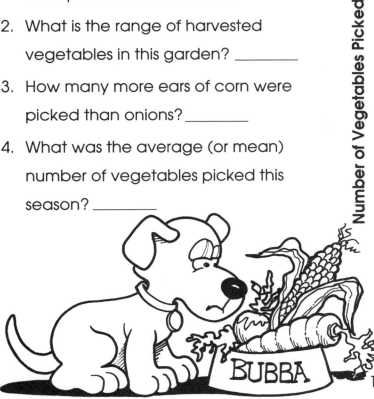

Dog Owners at Petumalot Elementary School

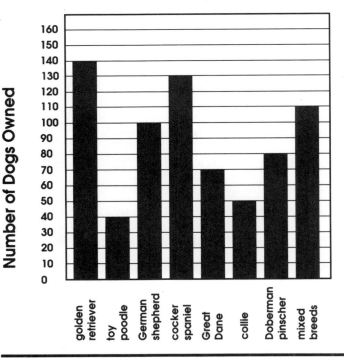

1. How many students own Great Danes at Petumalot Elementary School? _____

2. Which dog listed is owned by the least number of students? _____

3. Which breed is owned by the most number of students? _____

4. What is the mean number of dogs owned? _____

5. What is the range between golden retrievers and toy poodles? _____

6. How many students own Doberman pinschers? _____

7. How many more students own German shepherds than collies? _____

IF8747 Math Topics

Double Bar Graphs – I

Name _____

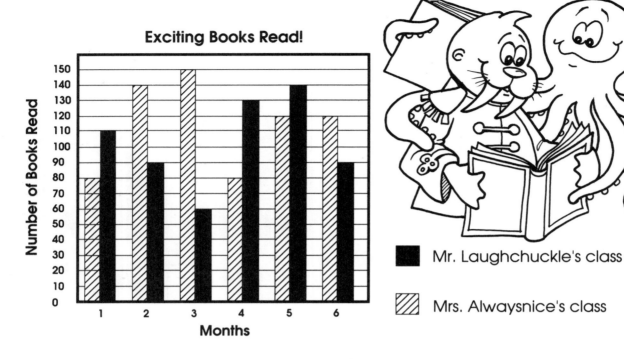

Exciting Books Read!

1. Which class read the most books during a one month period? _____
2. How many books in all did Mr. Laughchuckle's class read? _____
3. Which class read the most books during this six month period? _____
4. How many more books did Mrs. Alwaysnice's class read during month 3? _____
5. What was the mean number of books that Mrs. Alwaysnice's class read? _____

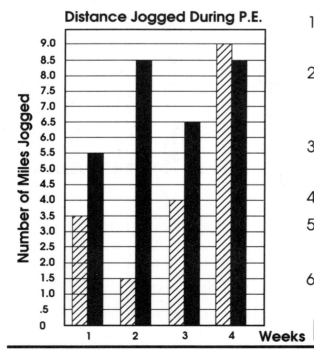

Distance Jogged During P.E.

1. Which class jogged the most during a one week period? _____
2. Which class jogged the most number of miles during this four week period? _____ What was the difference between classes? _____
3. Which week had the greatest range between the two classes? _____
4. Which week had the smallest range? _____
5. What was the mean number of miles jogged by Mrs. Singalot's class? _____
6. What was the range for Mr. Explainitwell's class during this four weeks? _____

Mr. Explainitwell's class   Mrs. Singalot's class

Double Bar Graphs – II

Name _____

Horseback Riders

Number of Hours Riding

12
11
10
9
8
7
6
5
4
3
2
1
0

Weeks
1 2 3 4 5

■ Michele

▨ Monica

1. Who rode the most of any given week? _____
2. What is the total number of hours that Michele spent horseback riding? _____
3. Which week did Monica ride the least number of hours? _____
4. Which week has the greatest range of hours between the two riders? _____
5. Who spent the most time horseback riding, Monica or Michele? _____

1. Which choir spent the greatest amount of time in rehearsal during the six week period?_____

2. What was the mean number of hours that concert choir spent in rehearsal? _____

3. In which two weeks did both choirs rehearse the same total number of hours? _____

4. Which choir rehearsed the least amount of time in a one week period? _____

5. Which choir rehearsed the greatest number of hours two weeks consecutively ? _____

Concert Choir Rehearsal Before the Big Performance!

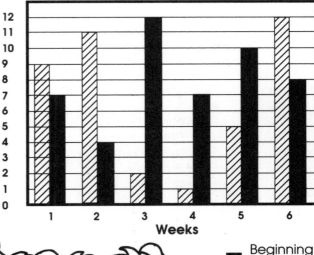

Number of Rehearsal Hours

12
11
10
9
8
7
6
5
4
3
2
1
0

Weeks
1 2 3 4 5 6

■ Beginning Choir

▨ Concert Choir

Pictographs

Name _____

Favorite Subjects in Science
(The Fifth and Sixth Grades at
Whataday Elementary)

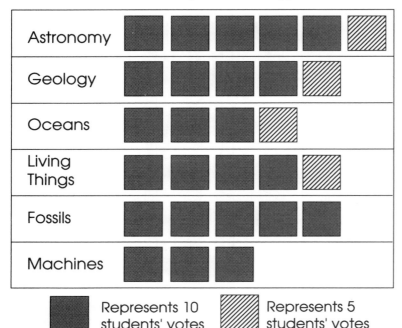

1. Which subject of science is the most popular at Whataday Elementary School? _____

2. Which one received the least number of votes? _____

3. How many students in all shared their opinion? _____

4. How many students in all voted for oceans and geology? _____

5. How many students said that the study of fossils was their favorite? _____

6. What is your favorite area in science? _____

7. If you asked the students in your class, what would the majority say is their favorite area in science? _____

Favorite Free Time Recreation
(The Fifth and Sixth Grades at Whataday Elementary)

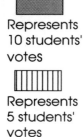

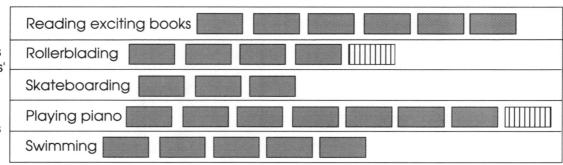

1. How many students voted for reading exciting books? _____
2. How many students voted for playing the piano? _____
3. Which activity received the greatest number of votes? _____
4. How many more votes did swimming receive than skateboarding? _____
5. How many students in all shared their opinion? _____
6. What is the range of votes on this pictograph? _____

Line Graphs

Name _____

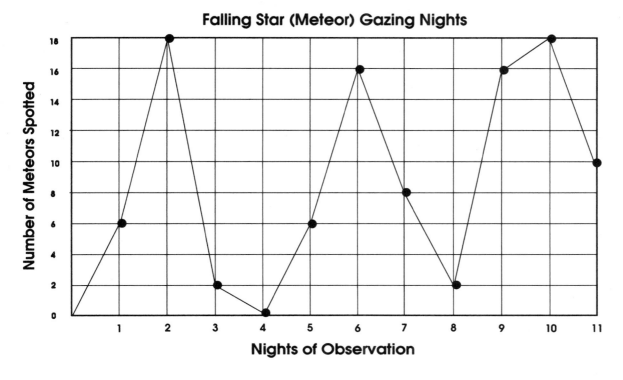

Falling Star (Meteor) Gazing Nights

1. How many more meteors were spotted on the second night than on the first? _____
2. How many nights were a total of 16 falling stars observed? _____
3. Which night were no meteors observed? _____
4. On which two nights were two meteors observed? _____
5. How many falling stars were observed altogether? _____

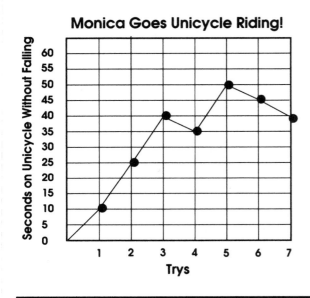

Monica Goes Unicycle Riding!

1. How many seconds was Monica able to stay balanced on her first try? _____

2. On her fourth try, was she able to stay on longer than her third try? _____

3. In all her times riding, which time did she stay on for the longest time? _____

4. What was the mean time that Monica remained on her unicycle? _____

5. Which time did Monica remain on her unicycle longer, the fifth or seventh try? _____

Double Line Graphs – I

Name _____

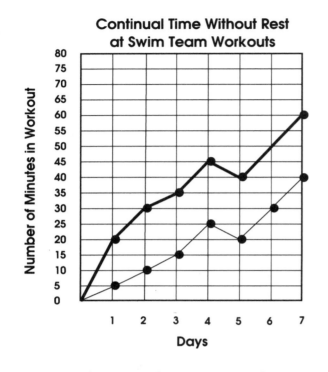

Continual Time Without Rest at Swim Team Workouts

Number of Minutes in Workout
80 75 70 65 60 55 50 45 40 35 30 25 20 15 10 5 0

Days
1 2 3 4 5 6 7

——— Cyndi swimming in week number 2
——— Cyndi swimming in week number 1

1. On the very first day of workouts, how soon after Cyndi started did she need to take a rest? _____

2. In week number one, how soon did Cyndi need to rest on day number three? _____

3. How long could she go without rest on the third day of the second week? _____

4. What is the range of week number one? _____

5. What is the range of week two? _____

6. Did Cyndi improve in both weeks? _____

Overseas Pen Pal Letters Received from France

Number of Letters
18 16 14 12 10 8 6 4 2 0

Months
Jan. Feb. Mar. April May June July Aug. Sept. Oct. Nov. Dec.

——— Mr. Shoe's class   – – – Mrs. Write's class

1. Which class received 18 letters more often within a one month period? _____

2. Which class received the most letters the first month? _____
   The last month? _____

3. How many letters did Mrs. Write's class receive in all? _____

4. Which class received more letters? _____

5. Which class only received two letters in January, May and December? _____

Double Line Graphs – II

Name _____

**Puppy Deliveries at
Dr. Barker's Office**

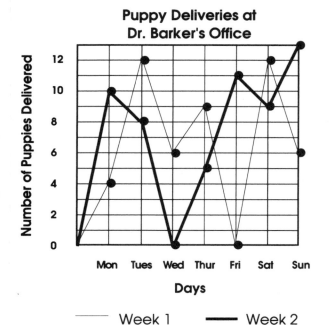

Number of Puppies Delivered

Mon Tues Wed Thur Fri Sat Sun

Days

——— Week 1   ■■■ Week 2

1. Which days did Dr. Barker not have to help deliver any puppies? _____

2. On which day and week were ten puppies delivered? _____

3. What was the mean number of puppies delivered in week one? _____

4. During week one, how many puppies were delivered on Saturday? _____

5. During week two, how many puppies were delivered on Sunday? _____

6. How many puppies has your friendly tail wagger delivered? _____

Back Yard Bird Feeders

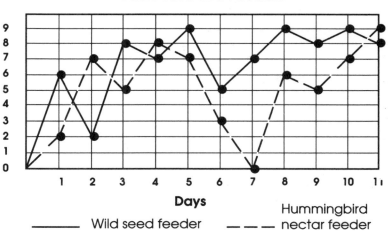

Number of Birds Seen Feeding

1   2   3   4   5   6   7   8   9   10   11

Days

——— Wild seed feeder   – – – Hummingbird nectar feeder

1. How many birds were seen munching on the wild seed on day number five? _____

2. How many hummingbirds were observed at the nectar feeder on day number seven? _____

3. How many days were a total of 9 birds seen eating at the wild seed feeder? _____

4. On day two, how many more hummingbirds were seen at the nectar feeder than the wild seed feeder? _____

5. Which feeder had more birds observed eating during this eleven day period? _____

Circle Graphs – I

Name _____

Lowell Lake's Busiest
Summer Recreation Spots

Total Visitors This Year: 15,300

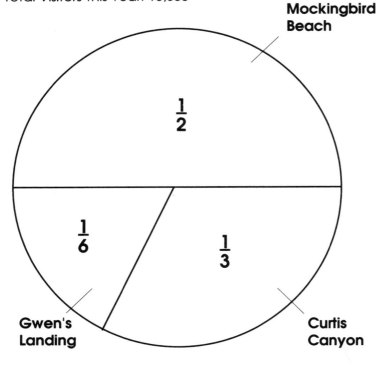

1. Which spot at Lowell Lake had the least amount of visitors?_____

2. How many people in all visited Mockingbird Beach? _____

3. What fraction of the people visited Gwen's Landing and Curtis Canyon combined?_____

Earlridge Community's Annual Food Drive

Total Pounds Collected: 183,200 pounds

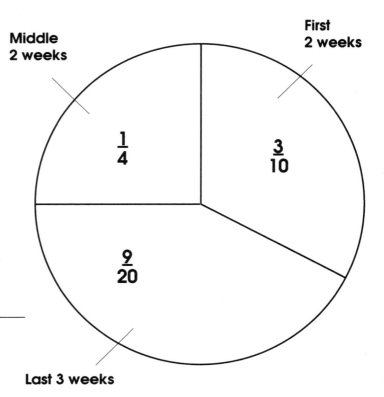

1. In which time period was the greatest amount of food collected?

   _____

2. How many pounds of food were collected in the first two weeks? _____

3. How many pounds of food were collected in the first four weeks? _____

4. In which time period was the least amount of food collected?_____

5. What fraction of the food was collected during the first two weeks and the last three weeks of the drive?_____

Circle Graphs – II

Name _____

**Students Vote for Lunch Entrees at
Sailboat Elementary School**

Total Votes Counted: 600

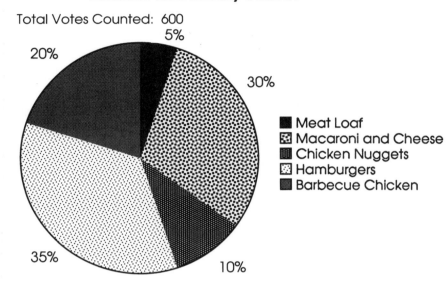

■ Meat Loaf
▦ Macaroni and Cheese
▓ Chicken Nuggets
▨ Hamburgers
■ Barbecue Chicken

1. Which entree received the most votes?_____
_____

2. How many votes were counted for meat loaf? _____

3. Which entree received the second most popular amount of votes?_____

4. How many students voted for barbecue chicken? _____

5. Which entree would have received the most votes if hamburgers and macaroni and cheese had not been listed in the poll? _____

6. Which entree would you have voted for? _____
Which one is the most popular at your school?_____

7. How many students at Sailboat Elementary School voted for chicken nuggets? _____

**Field Trips This Year in
Rollerblade Canyon School District**

Total Trips: 900

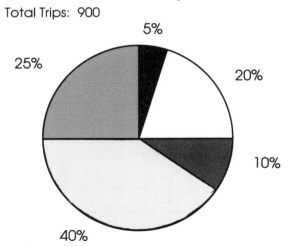

■ Out-of-state Adventures
☐ Overnight Camping
■ Symphony
☐ Wildlife Park and Zoo
▨ Museums

1. What percent of the students had the privilege of exploring in out-of-state adventures?

_____

2. How many field trips were taken to the symphony?

_____

3. Were more trips taken to the wildlife park and zoo, or to the museums and overnight camping combined? _____

4. How many overnight camping trips were taken? _____

Circle Graphs—III

Name _____

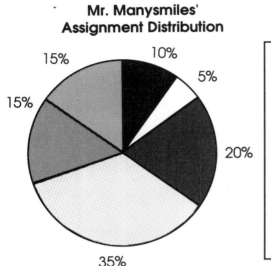

**Mr. Manysmiles'
Assignment Distribution**

15%   10%
15%   5%
15%   20%
35%

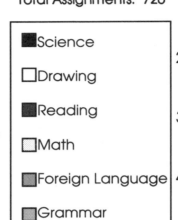

Total Assignments: 720

■ Science
□ Drawing
■ Reading
□ Math
▨ Foreign Language
▦ Grammar

1. How many reading and grammar assignments were given altogether? _____

2. What percent of the assignments were for science? _____

3. How many math assignments were given? _____

4. How many more foreign language assignments were given than drawing? _____

5. How many drawing assignments were given altogether? _____

6. What percent would have to be added to the number of science assignments given to equal those given in math? _____

7. If we add the reading and math assignments together, does this percentage equal more than the other subjects combined? _____

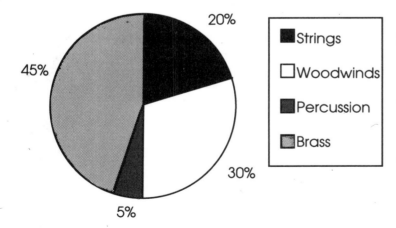

**Heather Cove Music Shop's Instrument
Rental's Since 1980**

Total Rentals: 23,760

20%
45%
30%
5%

■ Strings
□ Woodwinds
■ Percussion
▨ Brass

1. How many string instruments have been rented since 1980? _____

2. Which type of instrument has been rented the most? _____

3. Which instrument has been rented the least number of times? _____

4. How many string and woodwind instruments have been rented altogether since 1980? _____

5. If twice as many woodwinds had been rented than brass instruments, would this exceed the number of brass instruments rented? If so, by how many? _____

6. Which instrument do you play in your band or orchestra? _____

7. Which sounds the most beautiful to you? _____

Metric Units of Length - I

Name _____

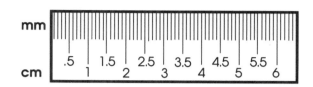

1 cm = 10 mm

Hint: If it's .5 or greater, round up to the next cm.
If it's less than .5, round down.

A. Complete each conversion.

30 mm = _____ cm	8.5 cm = _____ mm	50 mm = _____ cm
80 mm = _____ cm	38 mm = _____ cm	5.9 cm = _____ mm
14.2 cm = _____ mm	4.7 cm = _____ mm	900 mm = _____ cm
65 mm = _____ cm	3.2 cm = _____ mm	2.9 cm = _____ mm

B. Measure each section of this rocket in millimeters.

A = _____ mm
B = _____ mm
C = _____ mm
D = _____ mm
E = _____ mm
F = _____ mm
G = _____ mm

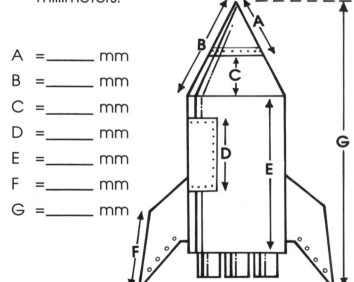

C. Measure each section of this hot air balloon to the nearest centimeter.

A = _____ cm
B = _____ cm
C = _____ cm
D = _____ cm
E = _____ cm
F = _____ cm

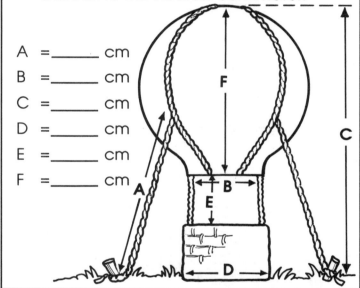

D. Measure in millimeters and to the nearest centimeter.

1. Width of your thumbnail – _____ mm _____ cm
2. Distance between your eyes – _____ mm _____ cm
3. Length of the pencil you're using right now – _____ mm _____ cm
4. Thickness of your front door – _____ mm _____ cm
5. Length of a book – _____ mm _____ cm
6. Length of a mailbox – _____ mm _____ cm
7. Width of your favorite photograph – _____ mm _____ cm
8. Length of your shoe – _____ mm _____ cm

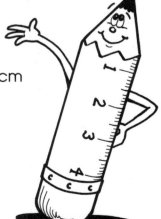

Metric Units of Length - II

Name _____

1 cm	=	10	mm
1 m	=	100	cm
1 km	=	1,000	m

A. Circle the appropriate metric unit for each measurement.

1. Distance from home to your school   **m**   **km**

2. Length of a piano keyboard   **cm**   **km**

3. Width of your refrigerator   **cm**   **m**

4. Thickness of your house key   **mm**   **cm**

5. Length of a dragonfly's wing   **mm**   **m**

6. Length of a cat's tail   **cm**   **km**

7. Length of a chalkboard   **m**   **km**

8. Distance you can kick a ball   **cm**   **m**

9. Height of a cloud in the sky   **mm**   **km**

10. Distance from the Earth to the sun   **m**   **km**

B. Circle the greater distance.

1. a. Jim's dog jumped 2 m as he crossed the creek!
   b. Monica's parakeet flew 284 cm from its perch to her finger.

2. a. David's model rocket flashed 42 m into the air.
   b. Andy and his family rafted 5 km down the river on Saturday.

3. a. Eva jogged a total of 6 km during P.E. this week.
   b. Bill's radio-controlled airplane flew 3,242 m.

4. a. Katelyn let out 600 cm of string before her kite took off!
   b. Sarah rode her unicycle 5.4 m before losing her balance!

5. a. The inchworm on Gwen's desk crawled 27 cm before disappearing.
   b. Cheryl's bean plant has already grown to be 306 mm tall.

6. a. Tom rode his rollerblades a total of 3 km yesterday.
   b. Mark painted 4 m of art work on the school walls this year.

Metric Units of Capacity

Name _____

$$1 \text{ mL} = 0.001 \text{ L}$$

A. Match each diagram with the correct capacity.

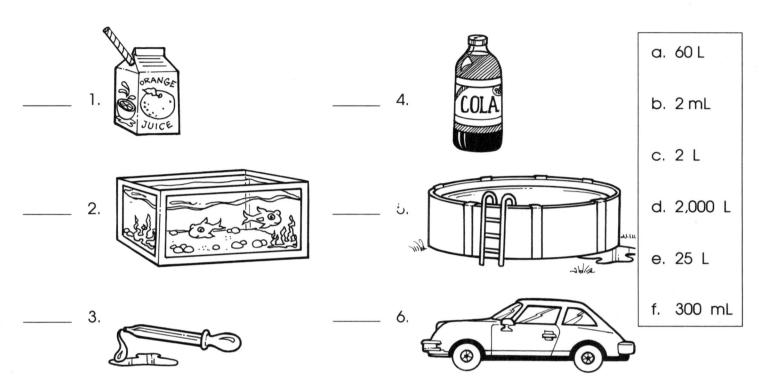

_____ 1.

_____ 2.

_____ 3.

_____ 4.

_____ 5.

_____ 6.

a. 60 L

b. 2 mL

c. 2 L

d. 2,000 L

e. 25 L

f. 300 mL

B. Circle the correct metric unit.

1. Michele's dad used 40 (**mL L**) of paint to cover the outside of their house.

2. Jeff filled his aquarium with 30 (**mL L**) of salt water.

3. After just a few days, 6 (**mL L**) of salt solution in a jar had evaporated.

4. Heather used 2 (**mL L**) of milk to make homemade ice cream!

5. Jolie found 320 (**mL L**) of grape juice included in her lunch.

6. Cindy used 10 (**mL L**) of cooking oil in the bread she was making.

C. Use a liter measuring cup to determine the capacity of each of these containers:

1. a can of soda – _____ mL

2. your favorite hot-beverage mug – _____ mL

3. a cereal bowl – _____ mL

Metric Units of Mass

Name _____

1,000 mg	=	1 g
1,000 g	=	1 kg

A. Astronauts aboard the spacecraft "Moon Crater" accidentally left the gravity machine off when they bunked down for the night. What mass would each of these floating items have on earth? milligram (**mg**), gram (**g**), or kilogram (**kg**)

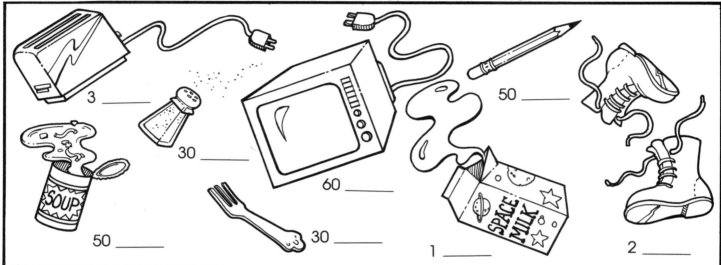

3 _____

30 _____

50 _____

60 _____

30 _____

1 _____

50 _____

2 _____

B. Solve the following problems.

1. Kelly's dog "Barksinger" weighs a total of 40 kg while soaking wet during a bath. After drying off, he loses 3,000 g. How much does Barksinger now weigh? _____

2. Carolyn picks 10 kg of oranges from her tree. After squeezing out the juice, she discovers that the leftover rinds weigh 2,000 g. How many kilograms of juice are there? _____

3. On Wednesday, Al ran a magnet through the sand to extract iron filings. He collected a total of 720 g of iron. On Thursday, he extracted another 1,280 g. How many kilograms did he extract altogether? _____

4. Marnie picked 82,000 g of watermelon for the family picnic. How many kilograms does this equal? _____

C. Circle the appropriate unit of mass.

1. Katy poured 350 (**mg   g   kg**) of salt on her steak.

2. Casandra lugged home 4 (**mg   g   kg**) of books in her backpack today.

3. Jonathan was pleased to find 10 (**mg   g   kg**) of black olives on his pizza.

4. Brittainy was happy to find that her new skates only weighed 2 (**mg   g   kg**).

Units of Length

Name _____

12 in. = 1 ft	5,280 ft = 1 mi
3 ft = 1 yd	1,760 yd = 1 mi

A. Complete.

9 ft = _____ yd   6 yd = _____ ft

3 mi = _____ yd   18 ft = _____ in.

3 mi = _____ ft   27 ft = _____ yd

39 in. = _____ ft _____ in.   5,280 ft = _____ mi

10,560 ft = _____ mi   6 ft = _____ in.

7 yd = _____ ft   144 in. = _____ ft

5 mi = _____ yd   48 in. = _____ ft

14 ft = _____ yd _____ ft   5,286 ft = _____ mi _____ yd

B. Measure each picture to the nearest eighth inch.

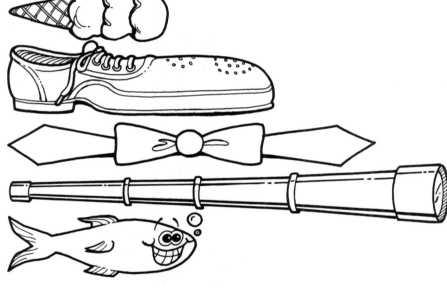

ice-cream cone: _____ in.

big shoe: _____ in.

long bow: _____ in.

telescope: _____ in.

very happy fish: _____ in.

A. Circle the correct unit of measure.

1. Width of a calculator is 3 (**in. ft yd mi**).

2. Length of your arm is _____ (**in. ft yd mi**).

3. Distance from one side of town to the other is 10 (**in. ft yd mi**).

4. Length of a guitar is 3 (**in. ft yd mi**).

5. The approximate distance from Earth to the planet Mars is 50,000,000 (**in. ft yd mi**).

6. Distance sound travels in one hour is approximately 750 (**in. ft yd mi**).

7. Distance light travels in one second is 186,000 (**in. ft yd mi**).

8. Distance from your feet to the top of your head is _____ (**in. ft yd mi**).

Units of Capacity

Name _____

A. Complete so that each row equals one gallon.

1. 3 qt + _____ qt = 1 gal

2. 4 c + 2 pt + _____ qt = 1 gal

3. 2 c + 1 pt + _____ qt = 1 gal

4. 3 qt + 2 c + _____ c = 1 gal

5. 2 pt + _____ qt + 1 qt = 1 gal

6. 6 c + _____ c + 2 qt = 1 gal

7. _____ qt + 2 c + 1 pt = 1 gal

1	pt	= 2 c
1	qt	= 2 pt
1	gal	= 4 qt

B. Match each equivalent capacity.

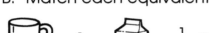 = 1 c 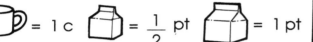 = $\frac{1}{2}$ pt  = 1 pt 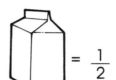 = 1 qt  = $\frac{1}{2}$ gal = 1 gal

1. _____

2. _____

3. _____

4.  _____

5. _____

a.

b.

c.

d.

e.

C. Which unit would best measure each example below?

1. Amount of water used to take a shower _____

2. Measuring flour to make bread _____

3. Filling your pool with water _____

4. A container of cottage cheese _____

5. A single serving of yogurt _____

6. A single serving container of milk from the store _____

7. A container of motor oil _____

gallons
cups
pints
quarts

Units of Weight

Name _____

1 lb	= 16 oz
1 T	= 2,000 lb

A. Complete.

32 oz = _____ lb   4 T = _____ lb

8,000 lb = _____ T   7 lb = _____ oz

60,000 lb = _____ T   3,000 lb = _____ T

32,000 oz = _____ T   240 oz = _____ lb

3 T = _____ lb   1,920 oz = _____ lb

96 oz = _____ lb $2\frac{1}{2}$ lb = _____ oz

48 oz = _____ lb $1\frac{3}{4}$ lb = _____ oz

1,000 lb = _____ T   5 lb = _____ oz

B. Circle the heavier amount.

1.	1 T	3,000 lb	6.	7 lb	113 oz
2.	3 lb	46 oz	7.	61,000 lb	30 T
3.	5,000 lb	2 T	8.	150 oz	9 lb
4.	6 T	11,000 lb	9.	2 lb 2 oz	35 oz
5.	64 oz	3 lb	10.	6 lb 4 oz	101 oz

C. Circle the correct unit of measurement.

1. Curt purchased 4 (**oz**   **lb**   **T**) of balsa wood to build his model airplane.

2. Diana and her friends collected 3 (**oz**   **lb**   **T**) of shells in 2 bags.

3. Mark and his family discovered that their furniture in the moving van weighed about 3 (**oz**   **lb**   **T**)!

4. Sharon purchased a 12 (**oz**   **lb**   **T**) bag of roasted peanuts at the circus.

5. Eva found that each of the baby rabbits in her back yard weighed 6 (**oz**   **lb T**)!

6. Chase carried the 10 (**oz**   **lb**   **T**) sack of apples up to the house.

7. Megan could not believe her mother had just purchased 70 (**oz**   **lb T**) of groceries at the store.

8. Crystal's brand new earrings weighed 3 (**oz**   **lb**   **T**).

Thermometers

Name _____

A. Identify each temperature in degrees Celsius (°C).

The boiling point of water	The freezing point of water	Our normal body temperature	A bird's body temperature	Freezer section of a grocery store

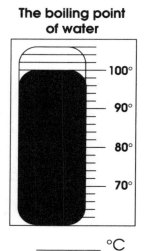 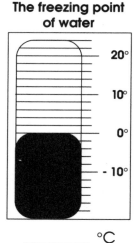 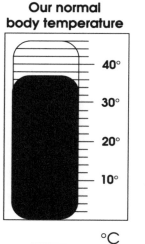 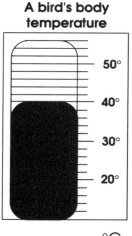 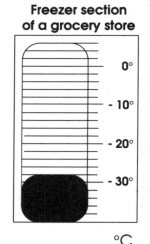

_____ °C   _____ °C   _____ °C   _____ °C   _____ °C

1. How many degrees Celsius does our body remain above the freezing point of water? _____

2. On the Celsius thermometer, how many degrees difference is there between the freezing and boiling points of water? _____

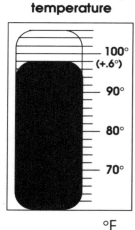

B. Identify each temperature in degrees Fahrenheit (°F).

A hot day in Phoenix!	A cold day in Vermont!	The boiling point of water	Our normal body temperature	Everything outside freezes!

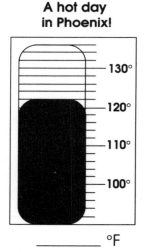 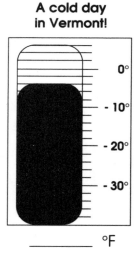 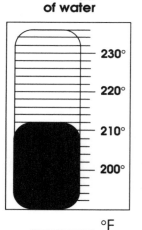 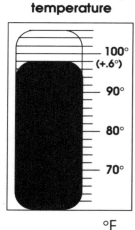 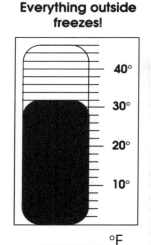

_____ °F   _____ °F   _____ °F   _____ °F   _____ °F

1. How many degrees difference is there on the Fahrenheit thermometer between the freezing and boiling points of water? _____

2. How many degrees difference is there between a hot day in Phoenix, AZ, and the boiling point of water? _____

Area

Name _____

A. Find the area of each figure.
   A = Length x width

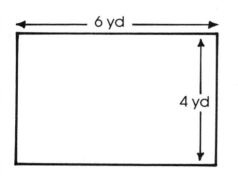

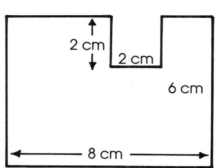

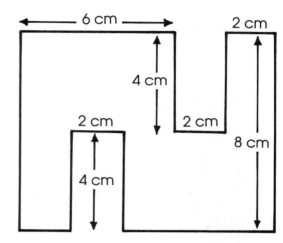

A = _____ yd²   A = _____ cm²   A = _____ cm²

B. Find the area of each triangle.
   A = 1/2 (b x h)

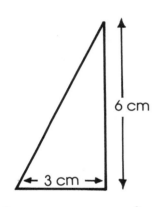

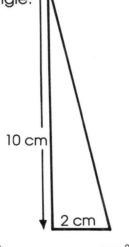

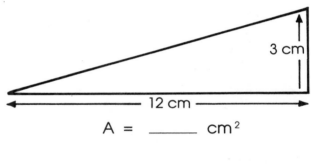

A = _____ cm²

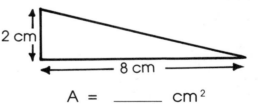

A = _____ cm²

A = _____ cm²   A = _____ cm²   A = _____ cm²

C. Find the area of each circle.
   A = π x r²   (π = 3.14)

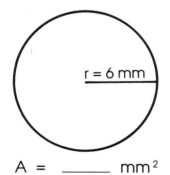

r = 6 mm

r = 8 cm

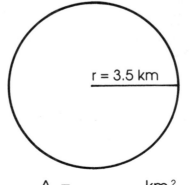

r = 3.5 km

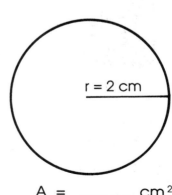

r = 2 cm

A = _____ mm²   A = _____ cm²   A = _____ km²   A = _____ cm²

Volume

Name _____

Find the volume of each figure.

$$V = \text{length} \times \text{width} \times \text{height}$$

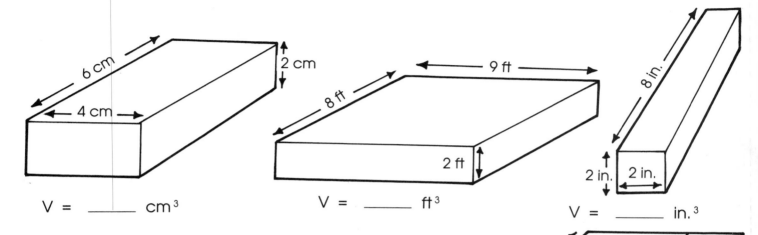

V = _____ cm³

V = _____ ft³

V = _____ in.³

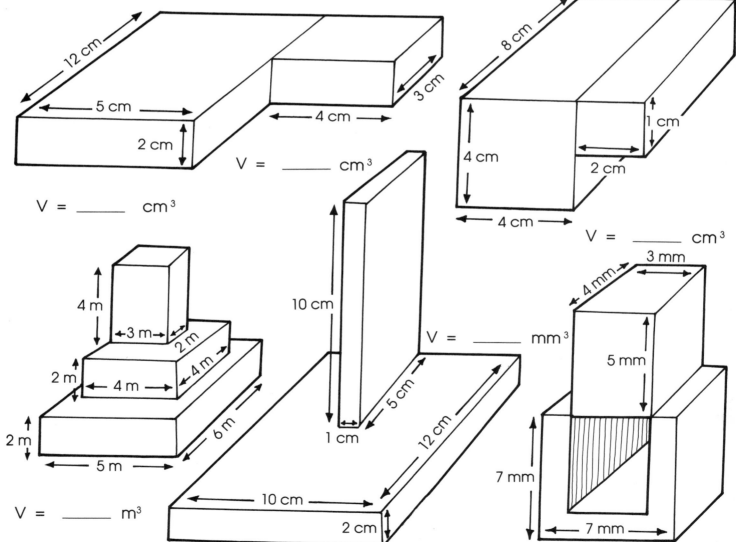

V = _____ cm³

V = _____ cm³

V = _____ cm³

V = _____ mm³

V = _____ m³

Points, Lines, Rays, Line Segments and Planes

Name _____

Match.

Point S = •S	Ray XY = $\overrightarrow{XY}$
Line CD = $\overleftrightarrow{CD}$	Line segment BC = $\overline{BC}$

1.  _____

2. Q _____

3.  _____

4.  _____

5. 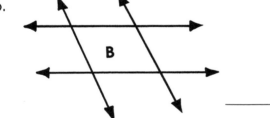 _____

6. 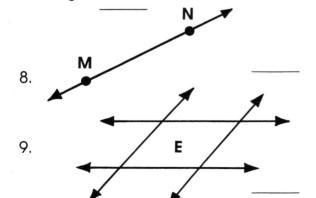 _____

7. X _____

8. _____

9. _____

10. 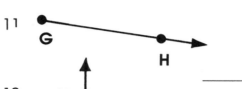 _____

11. _____

12. 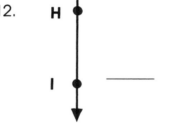 _____

13. A _____

14. 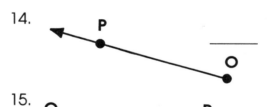 _____

15. 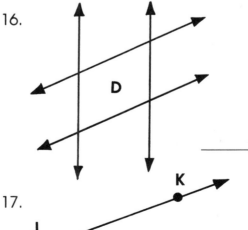 _____

16. _____

17. _____

A.	$\overrightarrow{GH}$
B.	Point Q
C.	Plane E
D.	Plane D
E.	Point A
F.	$\overrightarrow{OP}$
G.	$\overleftrightarrow{LM}$
H.	$\overline{YZ}$
I.	$\overleftrightarrow{MN}$
J.	$\overleftrightarrow{HI}$
K.	$\overrightarrow{JK}$
L.	$\overrightarrow{RS}$
M.	$\overleftrightarrow{PQ}$
N.	$\overrightarrow{TU}$
O.	Point X
P.	$\overline{QR}$
Q.	Plane B

Parallel, Intersecting and Perpendicular Lines and Line Segments

Name _____

$\overleftrightarrow{AB}$ is perpendicular to $\overleftrightarrow{CD}$ = $\overleftrightarrow{AB} \perp \overleftrightarrow{CD}$ $\overline{AB}$ is parallel to $\overline{CD}$ = $\overline{AB} \parallel \overline{CD}$

Circle the correct name for each figure.

1.
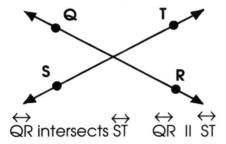

$\overleftrightarrow{QR}$ intersects $\overleftrightarrow{ST}$ $\overleftrightarrow{QR} \parallel \overleftrightarrow{ST}$

2.
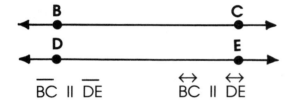

$\overline{BC} \parallel \overline{DE}$ $\overleftrightarrow{BC} \parallel \overleftrightarrow{DE}$

3.
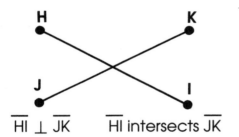

$\overline{HI} \perp \overline{JK}$ $\overline{HI}$ intersects $\overline{JK}$

4.
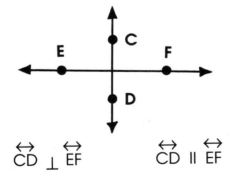

$\overleftrightarrow{CD} \perp \overleftrightarrow{EF}$ $\overleftrightarrow{CD} \parallel \overleftrightarrow{EF}$

5.

$\overleftrightarrow{EF}$ intersects $\overleftrightarrow{GH}$ $\overline{EF} \parallel \overline{GH}$

6.
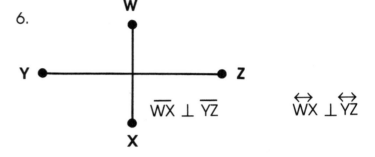

$\overline{WX} \perp \overline{YZ}$ $\overleftrightarrow{WX} \perp \overleftrightarrow{YZ}$

7.
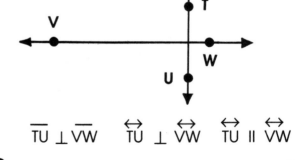

$\overline{AB}$ intersects $\overline{CD}$ $\overleftrightarrow{AB} \parallel \overleftrightarrow{CD}$

8.
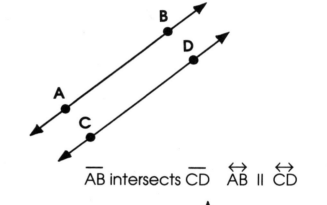

$\overline{TU} \perp \overline{VW}$ $\overleftrightarrow{TU} \perp \overleftrightarrow{VW}$ $\overleftrightarrow{TU} \parallel \overleftrightarrow{VW}$

9.
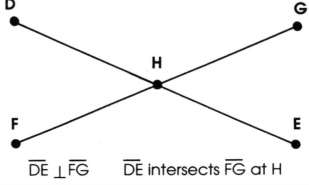

$\overline{DE} \perp \overline{FG}$ $\overline{DE}$ intersects $\overline{FG}$ at H

Working With Geometric Figures

Name _____

Use this figure to answer the questions below.

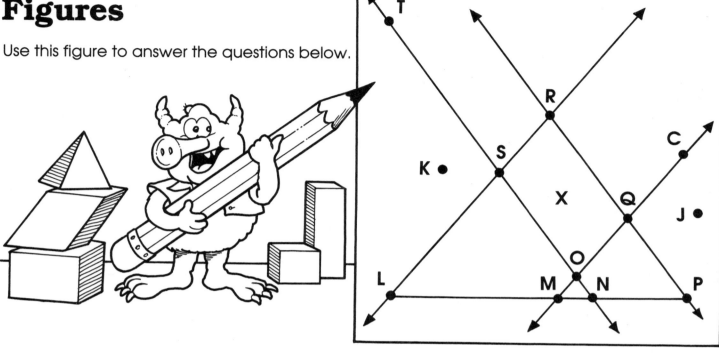

1. Name the plane in this figure. _____

2. Point K is inside which angle? _____

3. Name three triangles in this figure. _____

4. Point J is inside which angle? _____

5. Name three angles for which Q is the vertex. _____

6. Which points make up the parallelogram in this figure? _____

7. Name the largest triangle in this figure. _____

8. How many other angles can be named inside $\angle$ LNT? _____

9. Name all the angles that contain a side on $\overleftrightarrow{LR}$. _____

   _____

10. How many points are on $\overleftrightarrow{MC}$? _____ Name them. _____

11. Name the point at which $\overleftrightarrow{LR}$ and $\overleftrightarrow{NT}$ intersect. _____

12. Name the vertex for $\angle$ SNL. _____

13. Are lines $\overleftrightarrow{TN}$ and $\overleftrightarrow{RP}$ perpendicular or parallel? _____

14. Are lines $\overleftrightarrow{LR}$ and $\overleftrightarrow{MC}$ perpendicular or parallel? _____

Acute, Right and Obtuse Angles

Name _____

Acute Angle:	Less than 90°	Obtuse Angle:	Greater than 90°, less than 180°
Right Angle:	90°		

Label each angle.

1.

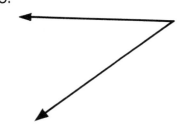

_____

2.

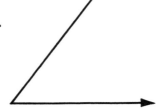

_____

3.

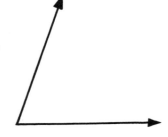

_____

4.

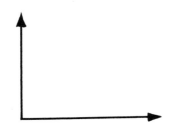

_____

5.

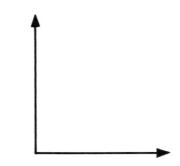

_____

6.

_____

7.

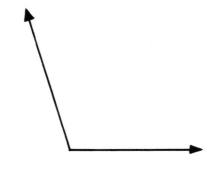

_____

8.

_____

9.

_____

10.

_____

11.

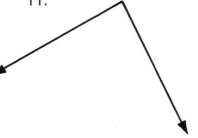

_____

12.

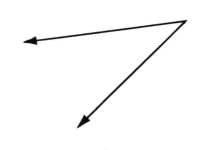

_____

Angle Measurement

Name _____

> The **degree** is the unit used to measure angles.

Measure the following angles using a protractor.

1. 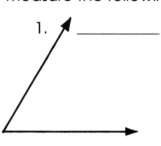 _____

2. _____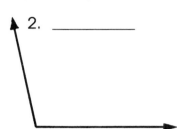

3. _____

4. _____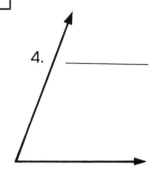

5. _____

6. _____

7. _____

8. _____

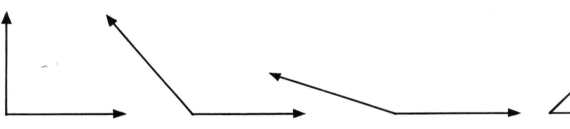

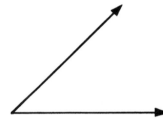

Draw the angles given using a protractor.

1. 70°

2. 120°

3. 40°

4. 90°

5. 150°

6. 110°

Congruent Figures – I

Name _____

Are these congruent? Write **yes** or **no**.

1.
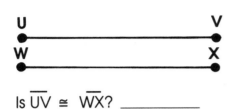

Is $\overline{UV} \cong \overline{WX}$? _____

2.
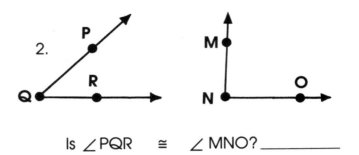

Is $\angle PQR \cong \angle MNO$? _____

3.
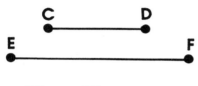

Is $\overline{CD} \cong \overline{EF}$? _____

4.
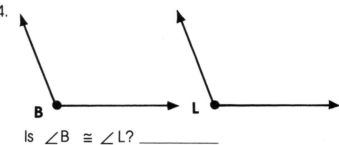

Is $\angle B \cong \angle L$? _____

5.
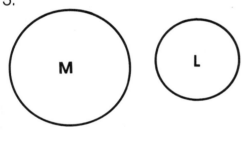

Is $M \cong L$? _____

6.
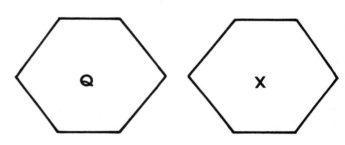

Is $Q \cong X$? _____

7.
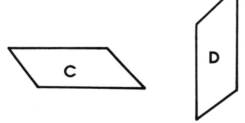

Is $C \cong D$? _____

8.
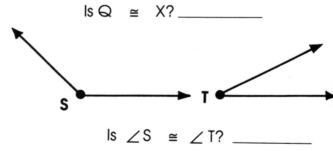

Is $\angle S \cong \angle T$? _____

9.
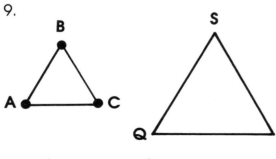

Is $\triangle ABC \cong \triangle QRS$? _____

10.
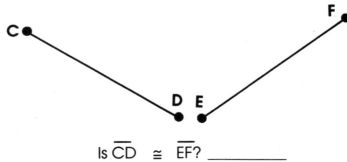

Is $\overline{CD} \cong \overline{EF}$? _____

Congruent Figures – II

Match the congruent figures.

Name _____

1. _____

2. _____
_____

3. _____

4. _____

5. _____

6. _____

7. _____

8. _____

9. _____

10. _____

11. _____

12. _____

13. _____

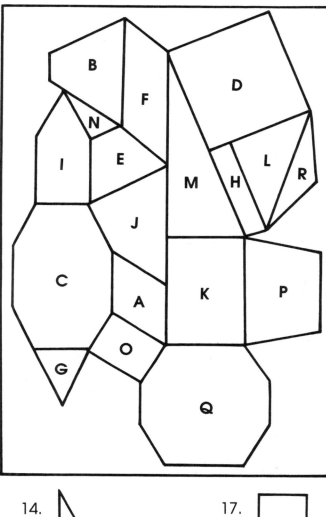

14. _____

15. _____

16. _____

17. _____

18. _____

IF8747 Math Topics

Symmetry – I

Name _____

A. Is the dotted line a line of symmetry?

1. _____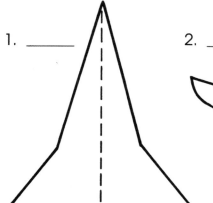

2. _____

3. _____

4. _____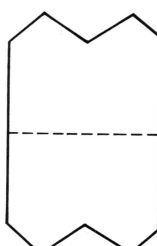

5. _____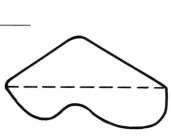

6. _____

7. _____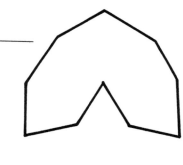

B. How many lines of symmetry are there in these figures?

1. _____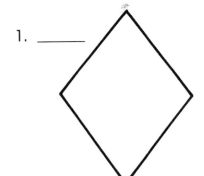

2. _____

3. _____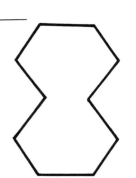

4. _____

5. _____

6. _____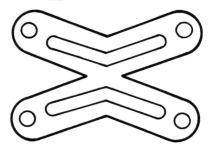

7. _____

Symmetry – II

Name _____

Draw the lines of symmetry.

Similar Figures

Name _____

Match the similar figures in the
Geometric Zoom Flasher photo!

1.  _____

2.  _____

3. 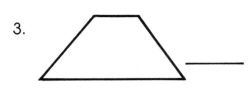 _____

4. _____

5. _____

6. 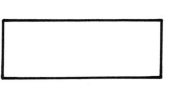 _____

7. _____

8. 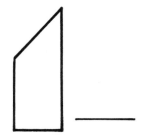 _____

9. 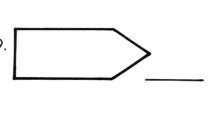 _____

10.  _____

Metric Match Magic

Name _____

100 centimeters (cm) = 1 meter (m)
1,000 meters (m) = 1 kilometer (km)

Match.

1.	2 m •	•	7 m	of
2.	900 cm •	•	600 cm	draw
3.	4,000 m •	•	500 cm	very
4.	700 cm •	•	200 cm	on
5.	3 km •	•	7,000 m	animal
6.	5,000 m •	•	5 km	paper
7.	6 m •	•	9 m	the
8.	2 km •	•	2,000 m	a
9.	800 cm •	•	4 km	back
10.	5 m •	•	3,000 m	this
11.	2,000 m •	•	8 m	magician's
12.	7 km •	•	2 km	favorite

Write the word beside each answer on the line. Then follow the directions.

1. _____ 2. _____ 3. _____ 4. _____ 5. _____

6. _____ 7. _____ 8. _____ 9. _____ 10. _____

11. _____ 12. _____

"Boxing" Match

Name _____

Step into the ring and figure the perimeter and area of each figure. Be a "knockout"!

☐ = 1 square inch

Example

Perimeter = __16__ in.

Area = __15__ sq. in.

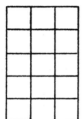

Perimeter = _____ in.

Area = _____ sq. in.

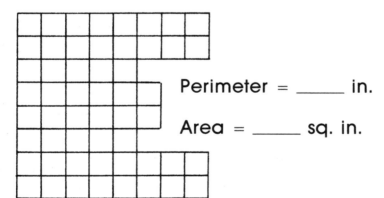

Perimeter = _____ in.

Area = _____ sq. in.

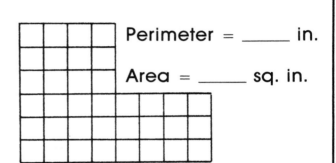

Perimeter = _____ in.

Area = _____ sq. in.

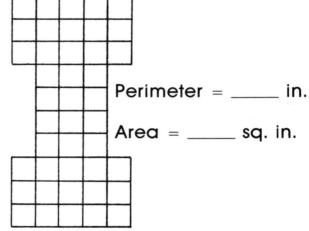

Perimeter = _____ in.

Area = _____ sq. in.

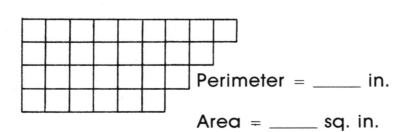

Perimeter = _____ in.

Area = _____ sq. in.

Perimeter = _____ in.

Area = _____ sq. in.

Yard Work

Name _____

1 ft. = 12 in.

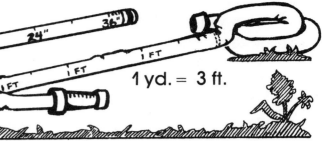

1 yd. = 36 in.

1 yd. = 3 ft.

Try this "yard" work by filling the blanks with "blooming" good answers.

3 ft. = __36__ in.	4 yd. = _____ in.	5 yd. = _____ ft.
6 ft. = _____ in.	7 yd. = _____ in.	9 yd. = _____ ft.
2 ft. = _____ in.	3 yd. = _____ in.	3 yd. = _____ ft.
4 ft. = _____ in.	5 yd. = _____ in.	7 yd. = _____ ft.
7 ft. = _____ in.	6 yd. = _____ in.	8 yd. = _____ ft.
5 ft. = _____ in.	8 yd. = _____ in.	4 yd. = _____ ft.

"Dig" deeper on these! Complete.

21 in. = _____ ft. and _____ in.	1 ft. and 4 in. = _____ in.
16 in. = _____ ft. and _____ in.	2 ft. and 6 in. = _____ in.
26 in. = _____ ft. and _____ in.	1 ft. and 10 in. = _____ in.
14 in. = _____ ft. and _____ in.	2 ft. and 8 in. = _____ in.

Name _____

Add or Subtract?

Learn these key words. They will help you know when to add and when to subtract.
Addition key words: **in all, altogether**   Subtraction key words: **more, left**
Circle the key words and solve the story problems.

1. Josh picked 47 quarts of strawberries. He sold 29 quarts. How many quarts of strawberries did he have left?

2. Josh sold 87 ears of corn and 115 apples. How many more apples than ears of corn did he sell?

3. Last week Josh made 436 sales. This week he made 367 sales. How many sales in all did Josh make?

4. On Tuesday Josh's sales amounted to $735.00. On Wednesday his sales amounted to $182.00. How much altogether did he sell in the 2 days?

5. Josh sold bananas for 39¢ per pound. He sold apples for 84¢ per pound. How many more cents per pound were apples than bananas?

6. Last week 212 of Josh's customers were women and 187 were men. How many customers did he have altogether?

7. Josh sold 178 quarts of blackberries and 69 quarts of raspberries. How many quarts of berries did he sell in all?

<u>Name</u>

Multiply or Divide?

Learn these key words. They will help you know when to multiply and when to divide.
Multiplication key words: **in all, altogether, times** and **each**
Division key words: **per ,each**

Circle the key words and solve the story problems.

1. There are 9 classrooms at the vocational school. The average number of students per classroom is 27 students. How many students altogether are there in the school?

2. 35 of the students are studying auto mechanics, and 3 times that many are studying business. How many students are studying business?

3. The semester is 16 weeks long. Students attend class 5 days a week. How many days in all must a student attend class each semester?

4. In one week an auto mechanics class installed a total of 63 new parts on 9 different cars. How many new parts is that per car?

5. In one class of 27 students, each student used $30.00 worth of materials. How much altogether did materials cost this class?

6. Lunch costs each student $11.50 for a 5-day week. How much does each lunch cost?

7. The average student drives a total of 8 miles per day to attend classes. How many miles in all does a student drive during the 80-day semester?

Name _____

Time — I

Fill in the clocks and solve the problems. The first one has been done for you.

1. Nita and Emily took part in the 12-mile Hunger Walk. They walked the 12 miles in 4½ hours. They finished at 4:00 p.m. At what time did they start?

4½ hours __Back__ = __11:30 a.m.__

2. After the 12-mile walk, Emily took a nap starting at 6:00 p.m. She awoke 8 hours later. At what time did she wake up?

8 hours __Forward__ = _____

3. Jerry slept in and started the 12-mile walk at 11:00 a.m. He walked across the finish line 5½ hours later. At what time did Jerry finish?

5½ hours _____ = _____

4. The first walker to finish the 12 miles crossed the finish line 3 hours after the official starting time of 10:00 a.m. At what time did the first walker finish?

3 hours _____ = _____

5. The last walker to finish the 12 miles started at 10:00 a.m. and finished 7½ hours later. At what time did this person finish?

7½ hours _____ = _____

6. Jill stopped for some water at 2:30 p.m. She had been walking for 3 hours. At what time had Jill started walking?

3 hours _____ = _____

7. The judges left the finish line at 5:30 p.m. They had started working 8 hours earlier. At what time did the judges start working?

8 hours _____ = _____

Name _____

Time — II

Solve the following problems.

1. 10:00 p.m. is Jeff's bed time. 8 hours later it is time for Jeff to get up. At what time does Jeff get up?

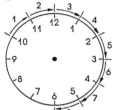

_____8_____ hours __Forward__ = __6:00__ a.m.

2. Afternoon classes start at 1:00 p.m. Morning classes start 4½ hours before the afternoon classes. At what time do morning classes start?

_____ hours _____ = _____

3. The school dance ended at 11:00 p.m., but it was 1:00 a.m. before Jane went to sleep. She slept only 6 hours. At what time did she get up?

_____ hours _____ = _____

4. Jeff had been in bed 5 hours when he had to get up at 2:00 a.m. to let his dog out. At what time had Jeff gone to bed?

_____ hours _____ = _____

5. The science teacher told the class to get up at 2:30 a.m., since that would be the best time to see the comet. At what time should the students go to bed in order to get 6 hours of sleep before 2:30 a.m.?

_____ hours _____ = _____

6. School was out at 3:00 p.m. Joe ran home to raid the refrigerator. He had not eaten since he had breakfast 8 hours before. At what time did Joe eat breakfast?

_____ hours _____ = _____

7. Ann's dog was happy to see her get off the school bus at 4:00 p.m. Her dog had not seen her since she left for school 8½ hours before. At what time had Ann left for school?

_____ hours _____ = _____

<u>Name</u> _____

Time — III

Solve the following problems.

1. Mary was out of bed at 6:30 a.m. She had lunch 6 hours later. What time did Mary have lunch?

   6 hours __Ahead__ = _____ p.m.

2. Mary returned from school at 4:00 p.m. Mary had left for school 8½ hours earlier. What time did Mary leave for school?

   8½ hours __Back__ = _____

3. Mary ate breakfast at 7:00 a.m. and ate dinner 11 hours later. What time did she eat dinner?

   11 hours _____ = _____

4. Mary started her homework at 7:30 p.m. and studied for 3½ hours. What time did she stop studying?

   3½ hours _____ = _____

5. On Saturday Mary was baby-sitting a neighbor's child. The parents returned at 3:00 p.m. They had been gone 5 hours. At what time did Mary start baby-sitting?

   5 hours _____ = _____

6. Mary's party started at 8:00 p.m. and was over 2½ hours later. Mary spent 1½ hours cleaning up after the last guest left. What time was Mary through cleaning?

   _____ hours _____ = _____

7. Mary's math class starts at 9:30 a.m. Her music class starts 4½ hours later. What time does Mary's music class start?

   _____ hours _____ = _____

8. School is out at 3:00 p.m. Baseball practice lasts 2 hours, and then the team takes ½ hour to shower and get dressed. What time does the team leave school?

   _____ hours _____ = _____

Name _____

More Than One Step — I

Solve the following problems.

1. Harvey took 12 cub scouts to the zoo. Admission to the zoo is $2.50 per person. He also bought each cub scout a 50¢ soft drink. What was Harvey's cost, not including his own admission, for this day at the zoo?

step 1:   **2.50**   step 2:   **12**   answer: _____

         +0.50   **x 3**

         3.00

2. The 12 cub scouts must each work on community projects at least 12 hours each month. What is the fewest number of hours altogether the cub scouts work on these projects in a year?

3. The scouts plan to have pancake breakfasts to raise money to buy new uniforms and to pay for a week at camp. Camp costs $35.00 per week for each scout. New uniforms cost $12.00 each. How much money must be raised for all 12 scouts to go to camp and for 6 scouts to get new uniforms?

4. A local car dealer loaned a van to the scout troop for the trip to camp. The van gets 14 miles per gallon of gasoline. Gasoline costs $1.10 per gallon. The trip to camp and back will cover 182 miles. How much will the trip cost in gasoline?

5. Food at the camp costs $5.25 per scout per day. How much will it cost to feed all 12 scouts for one week?

Name _____

More Than One Step — II

Solve the following problems.

1. The local police department has 52 members. ¼ of the police are women. ⅔ of the men are over 45 years of age. How many of the men are over 45?

   Step 1: 4 ⌐52   Step 2: 3 x _____ = _____

   Step 3: 3 ⌐‾   Step 4: 2 x _____ = _____

2. In one week the police investigated 4 times as many auto wrecks and fires combined as burglaries. They were called to 94 wrecks and 82 fires. How many burglaries did they investigate?

3. The police were called to investigate 42 fights where the people fighting were not related. They investigated 25 times that many family arguments. How many fights in all did the police investigate?

4. The police issued 480 parking tickets and 124 speeding tickets. "Driving under the influence" tickets totaled ¼ as many as the number of speeding tickets. How many tickets were issued in all?

5. Last week ¾ of the 124 speeders and ⅓ of the 72 jay walkers caught were second offenders and had to attend safety school. How many people altogether had to attend safety school?

6. The health insurance plan costs the city $27.00 per month for each of the 52 police force members. Life insurance costs ⅓ as much. How much is spent each year on insurance for the police force?

7. The city bought 7 new police cars that cost $16,500.00 each. 7 old police cars brought $3,400.00 each when traded in on new ones. How much was paid for the 7 new cars after the trade-in?

8. The banquet for 2 retiring police officers was attended by 250 local residents. Each resident paid $12.50 for the dinner. $500.00 of the money collected was spent on gifts for the retirees. How much was left to pay for the banquet?

More Than One Step — III

Solve the following problems.

1. Of 6 dinner guests, 2 ordered steaks at $15.95 each, 1 ordered flounder at $12.50 and the other 3 ordered shrimp at $9.95 each. What was their total bill?

   Step 1: 15.95   Step 2: 9.95
              x 2   x 3

   Step 3: + _____

2. At the next table, the waitress received orders for 2 soup-and-salad bars at $3.95 each and 2 sandwich-and-salad bars at $4.95 each. What was the total bill for this table?

3. The waitress served 3 other tables whose total bills were $62.90, $38.45 and $24.85. If each table tips her 15% of the total bill, how much in tips will the waitress receive?

4. For group parties 15% of the bill is automatically added as a tip. One party had a food bill of $382.50. Another party's bill came to ½ of that amount. How much in tips altogether did the waitress receive from these parties?

5. The restaurant is open 7 days each week. On an average day 250 cups of coffee are served at 60¢ per cup. How much money is collected for coffee each week?

6. The average lunch crowd has 84 guests ordering the soup-and-salad bar at $3.95 each. How much is spent for the soup-and-salad bar in a 7-day week?

7. During an average breakfast, 45 orders of pancakes and sausage at $3.25 each are filled. This amounts to how much money over 30 days?

8. The restaurant has 12 waitresses each receiving $4.00 per hour in wages. The rest of their pay comes from tips from the guests. Each waitress works 40 hours per week. How much in all does the management pay the waitresses each week?

<u>Name</u>

Multi-Step and Multi-Method

Solve the following problems.

1. Bill rides the bus to and from school each day. The bus fare is 20¢ each way. How much does Bill spend on bus fare during 20 days?

    step 1: **20¢ + 20¢** = _____

    step 2: **20 x (step 1)** = _____

2. Find another way to solve problem #1.

    step 1: **20 x 20¢** = _____

    step 2: **2 x (step 1)** = _____

3. Bill spends $2.75 for lunch at a fast food diner. Lunch in the school cafeteria costs $1.30. How much could Bill save by eating in the school cafeteria instead for 5 days?

    step 1:   step 2:

4. Find another way to solve problem #3.

5. The 5 girls each had a soft drink at 45¢ each and a bag of fries at 50¢ each. The 5 boys each had a soft drink at 55¢ each and ice cream at 70¢ each. How much more did the boys spend in all than the girls?

6. Find another way to solve problem #5.

7. It costs 4 times as much to outfit a football player as it does to outfit a basketball player. If it costs $260.00 to outfit one football player, how much more does it cost to outfit 10 football players than 10 basketball players?

<u>Name</u> _____

Something's Missing — I

Use this Table of Measures to help solve the problems on this page.

8 fluid ounces = 1 cup	2 pints = 1 quart	8 quarts = 1 peck	16 ounces = 1 pound
2 cups = 1 pint	4 quarts = 1 gallon	4 pecks = 1 bushel	2,000 pounds = 1 ton

1. The 5 pounds of hamburger needed for a cookout cost $5.60. How much does the hamburger cost per ounce?

   step 1: $5\overline{)5.60}$

   step 2: **1 pound** = _____ ounces

   step 3: $16\overline{)}$

2. A new tractor weighs 1¼ tons. How many pounds does the tractor weigh?

3. A gallon of ice cream sells for $3.20. How much will a 1-cup serving of ice cream cost?

4. 5 quarts of oil are needed for a car's oil change. How many oil changes can a mechanic make from a 50-gallon drum of oil?

5. Martha poured 24 cups of water into a jug. Her mother told her she needed 16 more cups of water to fill the jug. How many quarts will the jug hold?

6. A bushel of apples sells for $5.80. How much would a peck cost?

7. Bill sold a peck of strawberries at 85¢ a quart. How much money did he receive in all?

<u>Name</u>

Something's Missing — II

Use this Table of Measures to help solve the problems on this page.

100 centimeters (cm) = 1 meter (m)   10 decimeters (dm) = 1 meter (m)
1,000 meters (m) = 1 kilometer (km)   1,000 grams (g) = 1 kilogram (kg)

1. The label on the box listed the weight of the cereal at ⅛ kg. How many grams of cereal did the box hold?

2. Joan lives 1¼ km from school. Jane lives 845 m from school. How much farther is it from Joan's house to school than from Jane's house to school?

3. Amos swims 1,200 m each day. How many km does he swim in 30 days?

4. Clara learned to make 6 stitches per cm in her sewing class. The hem around her apron is 1¾ m. How many stitches are needed?

5. Al measured his flower bed and found it to be 18 dm long. Sue's flower bed is 3 m long. How much longer or shorter is Sue's flower bed than Al's?

6. The width of Henry's garden is 50 dm. The length of his garden is 40 m. The length of Henry's garden is how many times the width?

7. The tablecloth is 120 cm wide and 180 cm long. Will this cover a table 1 m wide and 1¾ m long?

Something's Missing — III

Some story problems seem to be missing information. Often the information can be found in a Table of Measures. Use this Table of Measures to help solve the problems on this page.

12 inches = 1 foot   1,760 yards = 1 mile
36 inches = 1 yard   5,280 feet = 1 mile
   3 feet = 1 yard

1. A farmer fenced in a field which was 657 feet long and 432 feet wide. How many yards of fence did he use?
Step 1: 3 feet = 1 yard   Step 2:

Step 3:

2. The fence was 3½ feet high. How many inches high was the fence?

3. The farmer walked around the boundaries of his farm. The farm is 740 yards long and 1020 yards wide. How many miles did the farmer walk?

4. The farmer walked 3½ miles looking for a lost calf. How many feet did he walk?

5. The trotting track is 880 feet around. The farmer rode the horse around the track 6 times. How many miles did he ride?

6. The distance from the house to the mailbox is 58⅔ yards. The farmer walks down to the mailbox and back to the house once every day. How many miles does he walk in 30 days?

7. Each time the tractor wheels turn over, the tractor has moved 6 feet. How many times will the wheels turn over in traveling 1 mile?

8. The farmer measures distance by pacing. Each step he takes is 1 yard long. How many steps will he take to pace off an area 42 feet by 36 feet?

Something's Missing — IV

Some story problems seem to be missing information. Often the information can be found in a Table of Measures. Use this Table of Measures to help solve the problems on this page.

60 minutes = 1 hour	8 fluid ounces = 1 cup
24 hours = 1 day	1 dozen = 12
52 weeks = 1 year	16 ounces = 1 pound
2 cups = 1 pint	
2 pints = 1 quart	
4 quarts = 1 gallon	

1. The clerk sold 5 dozen eggs for a total of $3.60. How much did each egg cost?

   Step 1: 1 dozen = 12   Step 2:

   Step 3:

2. A 1-gallon jug will hold how many cups of cider?

3. The clerk is paid $8.40 per hour. How much does he earn each minute he works?

4. A customer wanted 3¼ cups of syrup for a recipe. The syrup containers were marked in ounces. The clerk needed to look for a container which held how many ounces of syrup?

5. A 5-pound bag of sugar sells for $1.60. How much does each ounce of sugar cost?

6. The clerk has only 3 days of vacation left. How many minutes does he have before he has to go back to work?

7. A certain customer buys 1 pound of coffee every 2 weeks. How many pounds of coffee does this customer buy in one year?

8. One family buys 3 quarts of ice cream per week. How many cups of ice cream does this family eat each week?

Name _____

Too Much Information — I

Underline the **distractor** (unused fact) in each story and solve the problem.

1. Carl studied math for ¾ hour and then played with his dog for ½ hour before dinner. After dinner he studied 1½ hours for his other classes. How long altogether did Carl study?

2. Mr. Thomas teaches mathematics for 4½ hours each day and then spends 2½ hours each day coaching the basketball team. How much time does he spend on basketball in 5 days?

3. After school Marla spends ⅓ of her time practicing the piano, ¼ of her time on soccer practice and ⅙ of her time on voice lessons. What fraction of her time does Marla spend on music?

4. Mrs. Harper has 64 students in her choir. Of these students, ⅓ are boys. She also conducts the 48-member orchestra. How many music students does Mrs. Harper have in all?

5. In one class of 24 students, 8 are in the band and 12 are involved in athletics. What fraction of the class is in the band?

6. Mr. Wood works for 6 hours cleaning up after each ball game. Altogether, there are 34 ball games. Mr. Wood is paid at the rate of $6.00 per hour. How many hours in all does Mr. Wood spend cleaning up after ball games?

7. A year is 365 days long. Students spend 180 days a year in school. Each school day is 6 hours long. How many hours do students spend in school each year?

Too Much Information — II

Put a **distractor** in each of the following story problems and then solve the problems.

1. The pool is 12 feet wide and 25 feet long. Find the perimeter (distance around it).

   Add: The pool is 6 feet deep .

2. The pool is 25 feet long. How many laps (one length and back equals one lap) of the pool are equal to 100 yards?

3. It takes 4 hours for all the water in the pool to go through the filter. In 24 hours, how many times has the water been filtered?

4. Ann swam 10 laps of the 25-foot-long pool in 5 minutes. How many feet per minute did Ann swim?

5. Bill swam 1 mile (5,280 feet) in 15 minutes. How many feet per minute did Bill swim?

6. Bill, Joe, Chuck and Don each swam 12 laps of the 25-foot-long pool. How far did they swim altogether?

7. Mr. Long pays Bill $3.50 each day to clean the pool and check the chemicals. How much will Bill earn if the pool is open 110 days this summer?

Too Much Information — III

Underline the **distractor** (unused fact) in each story and solve the problem.

1. Bill is the sports writer for the school paper. He is allowed to use 2 pages for his articles. There are 32 lines of type on each page. The editorial section is 1 page long. The average line contains 16 words. How many words are there in Bill's sports section?

2. Bill wrote an article on basketball which took 12 lines. He wrote an article on intramural sports which took 14 lines. The average line contains 16 words. How many words were there in the basketball article?

3. Each page has 32 lines of type and 16 words per line. On one page Bill had an article covering 8 lines, using 128 words, and another article covering 11 lines. The rest of this page was to be used for a fan appreciation article. How many words could he use in the fan appreciation article?

4. Last week Bill attended 3 basketball games which each lasted 2 hours and 15 minutes. He averaged 28 minutes in writing about each of these events. How much time altogether did Bill spend attending sports events?

5. Bill spends 3 hours every school day attending sporting events and writing them up for the paper. He attends school from 8:00 a.m. until 3:00 p.m. How much time each week does Bill spend on his sports writing job?

6. The school paper has a staff of 12 people. Each time the paper is published, 14 spaces of advertising are sold for $7.50 each. How much is collected in a semester for advertising if the paper is published 12 times per semester?

7. Subscriptions to the paper sell for $2.50 for the 12 issues. Papers are sold at newsstands for 25¢ each. 430 subscriptions will bring in how much money?

8. The school paper staff was honored with a banquet. Besides the 12-member student staff, 134 adults attended. Banquet tickets cost $14.00 each. How much did the adults pay in all?

Name _____

Too Much Information — IV

Put a distractor in each of the following
problems and then solve the problem.

---

1. Mr. Johns is placing stepping-stones
   across his garden. Each stepping-stone
   costs $1.25.
   The stones will be placed 6 inches apart.
   (distractor)
   How much will 12 stones cost?

2. Mr. Johns bought a garden tractor for
   $564.00 and used it for 12 years. _____
   _____
   How much did each year of use cost?

---

3. The 14 flowering shrubs for Mr. Johns's
   garden cost $9.60 each. _____
   _____
   How much did the shrubs cost altogether?

4. Putting an ornamental fence around the
   garden, which is 37 feet long and 27 feet
   wide, will cost $18.00 for each 4-foot
   section. _____
   _____
   How much will the fence cost?

---

5. It took 2 children 14 hours to paint the
   fence. Mr. Johns paid them each $3.25
   per hour. _____
   _____
   How much altogether did he pay the
   fence painters?

6. For his garden, Mr. Johns bought a picnic
   table for $42.95, 4 benches at $14.49
   each and 6 chairs at $12.25 each. _____
   _____
   How much did he spend altogether?

---

7. A charcoal grill cost $19.95. It cost Mr.
   Johns $112.00 to build a brick enclosure
   for it. _____
   _____
   How much did the grill and the enclosure
   cost altogether?

8. Mr. Johns bought a bug light for $28.95
   and 3 cans of insect spray that cost $4.35
   each. _____
   _____
   How much did Mr. Johns spend on insect
   control?

Name _____

Too Much or Not Enough? — I

Each of the following problems contains too much or too little information. If too much information is given, underline the distractor and solve the problem. If not enough information is given, write "NE."

1. Chuck has 6 rows across the garden for every 5 feet of space. How many rows in all are in his garden?

2. Chuck has 3 times as many rows of beans as peas, and he has 4 times as many rows of potatoes as peas. He has 3 rows of peas. How many rows of beans are there in Chuck's garden?

3. Cucumber plants produced an average of 18 cucumbers per hill. 5 of the cucumbers weighed one pound each. There were 12 hills altogether. How many cucumbers were produced in all?

4. Chuck had 49 potato plants. The average potato weighed 1¼ pounds. How much did the potatoes weigh altogether?

5. Chuck paid Bill $3.50 per hour to help him in his garden. Bill dug potatoes for 7 hours and picked beans for 1½ hours. How much did Chuck pay Bill to dig potatoes?

6. Potatoes sell for $2.79 per 10-pound bag. Chuck bagged potatoes for 6 hours. How much money did he make?

7. Chuck sold $4.50 worth of green beans and $2.70 worth of tomatoes. At 30¢ per pound, how many pounds of green beans did Chuck sell?

<u>Name</u> _____

Too Much or Not Enough? — II

Each of the following problems contains too much or too little information. If too much information is given, underline the distractor and solve the problem. If not enough information is given, write "NE."

1. An Earth day is 24 hours long. A day on Mars is equal to 25 Earth hours, while a day on Mercury is equal to 2,100 Earth hours. How many times as long as a day on Mars is a day on Mercury?

2. A year on Earth is 365 days long. A year on Mercury is equal to 88 Earth days. A year on Pluto is equal to 248 Earth years. How many more Earth days are there in an Earth year than in a Mercury year?

3. A day on Earth is 24 hours long. A Uranus day is shorter than an Earth day. How many hours are there in a Uranus year?

4. An Earth day is 24 hours long. A Pluto day is equal to 140 Earth hours. A Pluto year is equal to 248 Earth years. How many Earth hours less is 30 days on Earth than 7 days on Pluto?

5. Venus's day is equal to 5,400 Earth hours. An Earth year is 365 days long. An Earth day is 24 hours long. A Venus day is how many times as long as an Earth day?

6. An Earth day is 24 hours long. A Mercury day is equal to 2,100 Earth hours. A Pluto day is equal to 140 Earth hours. A Mercury day is how many times as long as a Pluto day?

7. An Earth day is 24 hours long. A day on Saturn is equal to 10 Earth hours. A Mars day is how many times as long as a day on Saturn?

Too Much or Not Enough? — III

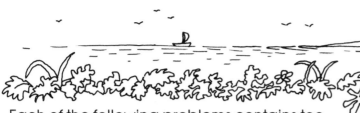

Each of the following problems contains too much or too little information. If too much information is given, underline the distractor and solve the problem. If not enough information is given, write "NE."

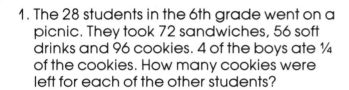

1. The 28 students in the 6th grade went on a picnic. They took 72 sandwiches, 56 soft drinks and 96 cookies. 4 of the boys ate ¼ of the cookies. How many cookies were left for each of the other students?

2. One of the girls baked half of the cookies. Two boys baked the rest of the cookies. The girl who baked half the cookies spent $5.00 on ingredients. How much did she spend on flour?

3. The 56 soft drinks cost 22¢ each. The sandwiches cost 85¢ each to make. How much was each of the 28 students' share of the soft drink cost?

4. If the sandwiches had been bought at a deli, the cost for each sandwich would have been 3 times the cost for making each sandwich at home. How much would 72 sandwiches cost at the deli?

5. The students drank 75% of the 56 soft drinks and ate ⅚ of the 72 sandwiches. How many sandwiches were left uneaten?

6. The school is ¾ mile from the park. The 16 students whose parents did not pick them up at the park walked home. How far altogether did these students walk?

7. Of the 28 students, 1 student did not enjoy the picnic. Of the rest of the class, ⅔ want to have another picnic soon. 9 students said they enjoyed it but did not want another picnic for a while. How many students want another picnic soon?

8. Of the 28 students, all but 4 live in town. ⅚ of those living in town walk to school. Some students ride their bikes to school. How many students are brought to school by their parents?

Too Much or Not Enough? — IV

Each of the following problems contains too much or too little information. If too much information is given, underline the distractor and solve the problem. If not enough information is given, write "NE."

1. The local high school has won 85% of its basketball games and 60% of its football games over the last 10 years. How many of the school's 220 basketball games has it won?

2. The wrestling team has won ¾ of its 28 matches over the last 2 years, and the football team has won 70% of its games over the last 2 years. How many games did the football team win?

3. There are 8 members on the tennis team. There are 3 times as many basketball players as tennis players. 3 times as many students play football as play basketball, and 1½ times as many students play baseball as play basketball. Altogether, how many students play basketball and baseball?

4. The boys' basketball team has won 340 more games than it has lost over the past 20 years. What percentage of its games has the team won?

5. The gym seats 4,500 fans. The first game of the season was sold out. For the last game of the season there were 1,250 empty seats. Tickets for adults cost $2.50 each. Student tickets cost $1.25 each. How much money was collected for the first game of the season if 2,200 of the fans were students?

6. The wrestling team had 127 fans who each paid $1.50 to attend the first meet. 246 people each paid $1.50 to see the last meet. How much money was collected at the last meet?

7. The total attendance for the 5 home football games was 33,000. The total attendance for the 89 home wrestling meets was 1,650. What was the average attendance at each of the football games?

8. Of the school's 180 athletes, ⅔ plan to attend college. Of the entire student body, 40% plan to attend college. How many of the athletes plan to go to college?

Write Your Own Problem

Solve each problem. Then write a new question for each one so that you have a different story problem. Next solve your own problem.

1. A building contractor pays a carpenter $12.00 per hour and a carpenter's helper $8.00 per hour. In a 40-hour week, how much does the contractor pay the carpenter and his helper altogether?

Solution:

New Question:
In a 40-hour week, how much does the carpenter's helper earn?

New Solution:

2. Last year the contractor paid $124,800.00 in wages to his employees. $\frac{3}{5}$ of the wages went to the carpenters. The rest of the wages went to the carpenters' helpers. How much altogether were the carpenters paid last year?

Solution:

New Question:

New Solution:

3. The contractor was paid $340,000.00 to build a commercial building. He paid $31,200.00 to his employees in wages, $920.00 for employee fringe benefits, $1,800.00 for office costs and $210,000.00 for materials. How much profit did he make off of this job?

Solution:

New Question:

New Solution:

4. A garage was built in 4 workdays of 8 hours each by 2 carpenters and 1 helper. The carpenters were each paid $12.00 per hour, and the helper was paid $8.00 per hour. How much in wages did building this garage cost?

Solution:

New Question:

New Solution:

5. Last year the contractor built and sold 23 houses for a total profit of $183,000.00. However, he built 7 more houses which sold at a loss of $4,300.00 each. What was his overall profit from building houses?

Solution:

New Question:

New Solution:

6. Altogether, the contractor made a profit of $243,000.00 last year. He gave $27,000.00 to local charities and $24,300.00 to a church. How much more than 15% of his profit did he give away?

Solution:

New Question:

New Solution:

Name _____

You Can Do It! — I

Solve the following problems.

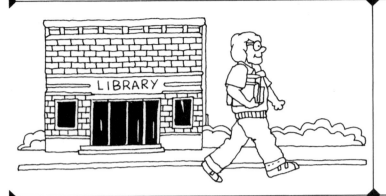

1. The school is ⅝ mile from Jack's house. How many miles does Jack ride his bike to and from school in 5 days?

2. The library is 2¼ miles farther from Jack's house than the school is. The school is ⅝ mile away. How far does Jack live from the library?

3. The library is 2¼ miles from Jack's house. The ice cream parlor is ½ mile farther down the street. How far has he pedaled his bike if he goes to the library, then to the ice cream parlor, and then back home?

4. Jack lives 12 miles from the ball park. He can pedal his bike 10 miles in 30 minutes. How long will it take Jack to ride his bike to the ball park?

5. It takes 4 trips around the track to make a mile. Jack pedaled his bike around the track 24 times. It took him 30 minutes. How many miles per hour was Jack pedaling?

6. It takes Jack 15 minutes to walk a mile. It takes Jack 4 minutes to ride his bike a mile. How much farther can he ride his bike than he can walk in one hour?

7. Jack rode his bike for 2⅓ hours at a speed of 12 miles per hour. The next 1½ hours his speed dropped to 10 miles per hour. How many miles did he cover altogether?

 IF8747 Math Topics

Name _____

You Can Do It! — II

Solve the following problems.

1. The club has 120 members. It costs each member $200.00 to join, and the annual dues are $60.00 per member. How much is collected in dues each year?

2. Dinner at the club costs $12.00 per person. Lunch at the club costs $4.00 per person. If a member ate dinner at the club 38 times during one year, how much would these dinners cost in all?

3. The dining room at the club is 38 feet long and 22 feet wide. 96 diners can be seated at one time. If ¾ of the 120 members come to dinner and each brings a guest, how many must wait for the 2nd seating?

4. If 96 members eat dinners that cost $12.00 each, how much in all will these dinners cost?

5. One day ¼ of the 120 members ate the $4.00 lunch, and ½ of the 120 members ate the $12.00 dinner. Altogether, how much more was spent for dinner than for lunch?

6. The annual Halloween party is free for members wearing costumes. A $5.00 admission fee is charged those not in costume. ⅕ of the 120 members were not in costume. Altogether, how much did these members pay?

7. A $25.00 per person admission is charged for the Christmas party, and the money is used to buy gifts for children. Members and guests attending the party totaled 180. How much money was collected?

You Can Do It! — III

Study each problem carefully and find the solution.

1. Mary has 40 books in her library. She has read them all. The average book has 180 pages. How many pages has she read?

2. Mary reads 1 page in about 4 minutes. How many hours would it take Mary to read a book with 240 pages?

3. Reading at the rate of 4 minutes per page, how many days would it take Mary to read all 40 of her books, each containing 180 pages, if she reads 6 hours each day?

4. The average page contains 30 lines, and the average line contains 12 words. If Mary reads a page in 4 minutes, how many words per minute is she reading?

5. One of Mary's books containing 240 pages has how many words if there are 390 words per page?

6. It takes Sherry ¾ as long to read a page as it does Mary. Mary reads a page in 4 minutes. How many hours would it take Sherry to read a 240-page book?

7. Mary's book has 600 pages, and Sherry's book has 620 pages. Mary reads at a rate of 4 minutes per page, and Sherry reads at a rate of 3 minutes per page. How many more hours will it take Mary to read her book than it will take Sherry to read her book?

8. The fastest reader in the 6th grade reads 160 words per minute. How long would it take this student to read a 200-page book which has 12 words per line and 30 lines per page?

You Can Do It! — IV

COST 16¢
PROFIT 34¢

ICE CREAM

Study each problem carefully and find the solution.

1 pint = 2 cups
2 pints = 1 quart
4 quarts = 1 gallon

1. The 6th grade class is making ice cream for the school carnival. The class estimates that 448 people will buy ice cream. If 1 cup of ice cream is served to each person, how many gallons of ice cream will be needed?

2. One gallon of ice cream takes 3 eggs, 1 pound of sugar and ¾ quart of cream. Eggs cost 84¢ per dozen, a 5-pound bag of sugar costs $2.00, and cream sells for $2.60 per quart. What is the cost of making a gallon of ice cream?

3. Each 1 cup serving of ice cream will sell for 50¢. How much profit is made from the sale of each gallon of ice cream? (See problem #2 result.)

4. If 448 servings of ice cream are sold at 50¢ each, how much money in all is received from the sale of the ice cream?

5. If each serving costs 16¢ to make and is sold for 50¢, how much profit is made from 25 servings?

6. If the profit on each serving of ice cream is 34¢, and the 6th grade class sold 448 servings, how much profit did the class make?

7. The 28 students each worked 2½ hours while making the ice cream and setting up the booth. They each worked ¾ of an hour during the carnival. In all, how many hours did the class work?

8. The 5th grade basketball toss was a much more profitable project. They made 3 times as much money as did the 6th grade project. How much did the 5th grade make? (See problem #6 result.)

Problem Solving Review

Solve the following problems.

1. It is a distance of 1,037 miles from Boston to Atlanta. The distance from Boston to Cheyenne is 870 miles farther than it is from Boston to Atlanta. How many miles is it altogether from Boston to Cheyenne?

2. It is 3 times as far from Austin to Des Moines as it is from Indianapolis to Cleveland. It is 294 miles from Indianapolis to Cleveland. How many miles is it from Austin to Des Moines?

3. It is 941 miles from Fort Worth to Chicago and 757 miles from Forth Worth to Denver. How many more miles is it from Fort Worth to Chicago than it is from Forth Worth to Denver?

4. The distance from Knoxville to Los Angeles is 2,198 miles, which is 7 times the distance from Cleveland to Harrisburg. How many miles is it from Cleveland to Harrisburg?

5. It is ¼ as far from Washington, D.C., to Detroit as it is from Washington, D.C., to Salt Lake City. It is 2,044 miles from Washington, D.C., to Salt Lake City. How many miles is it from Washington, D.C., to Detroit?

6. A trip from Detroit to Chicago and then to Milwaukee is a distance of 353 miles. It is a distance of 266 miles from Detroit to Chicago. How many more miles is it from Detroit to Chicago than it is from Chicago to Milwaukee?

7. The distance from Atlanta to New Orleans is 482 miles. It is 2 times as far from Atlanta to New Orleans as it is from Atlanta to Nashville. How many miles is it from Atlanta to Nashville?

8. It is 3 times as far from Minneapolis to New Orleans as it is from Minneapolis to Chicago. The distance from Minneapolis to New Orleans is 1,215 miles. How many miles is it from Minneapolis to Chicago?

Blast Off!

Study each problem carefully and then find the solution.

1. The 6th grade class has decided to hold a class reunion in space during the year 2010. The first stop will be on the Earth's moon, which is 240,000 miles from Earth. If the trip to the moon takes 3 hours, how many miles per hour will they be traveling?

2. The next stop of the class reunion will be on Mercury, where everyone will wish to be weighed. On Mercury your weight is only ¼ of your weight on Earth. How much would a 256-pound Earthling weigh on Mercury?

3. Earth is 93,000,000 miles from the sun. Mercury is ⅖ as far from the sun as Earth is. How far is Mercury from the sun?

4. On Mars your weight will be 0.38 times your Earth weight. How many pounds will a 200-pound Earthling weigh on Mars?

5. Mars is 1½ times as far from the sun as Earth is. Earth is 93,000,000 miles from the sun. How many miles is it from Mars to the sun?

6. From Mars the group will travel to Jupiter, a distance of 998,000,000 kilometers. In the year 2010, the students' trip to Jupiter will take 40 days. How many kilometers will they be traveling per day?

7. The group probably will not visit Pluto because traveling there would take about 8 months. It is 3,600,000,000 miles from Earth to Pluto. To make the trip in 8 months, the spaceship would have to travel how many miles per month?

8. Isaac Newton was born in 1642. Twenty years later he discovered the law of gravity. In the year 2010, the former 6th graders will discover that Newton's law of gravity is still true. In the year 2010, how many years will it have been since Newton discovered the gravitation law?

Mean Monster's Way-out Weigh-in

Name _____

Mean Monster is a fifth grader who plays football for the OKI-DOKI OUTLAWS. He now weighs 519 pounds and stands 7 feet 5 inches tall. He has only three teeth left, and his nose has been broken four times. He has some trouble in school. Can you help him figure out these math problems?

Work the problems on another paper.

Answer Space

1. Mean Monster's little brother Itty Bitty Monster weighs only 338 pounds. What is the difference in their weights?

2. Mean Monster stood on the school scale with his brother Itty Bitty. What was their total weight?

3. Mean Monster always eats his vegetables. In fact, he ate 192 ounces of mashed potatoes and gravy. There are 16 ounces in each pound. How many pounds of mashed potatoes did he eat?

4. Mean Monster ate 7 pounds of hamburger at one meal. How many ounces of meat did he eat?

5. Mean Monster's best friend Bonebasher weighs 463 pounds. How much less than Mean Monster does Bonebasher weigh?

6. Mean Monster, Itty Bitty Monster and Bonebasher all stood together on the school scale. What was their total weight?

7. Mean Monster's dad weighs 3 times as much as he does. What is his dad's weight?

8. Itty Bitty Monster ate 256 ounces of food for his lunch. How many pounds of food was that?

9. There are 16 ounces in a pound. Help Mean Monster figure out how many ounces he weighs.

10. Tony is a fifth grader who weighs 73 pounds. How much more does Mean Monster weigh?

Buggs I. Lyke Serves Lunch

Name _____

Buggs I. Lyke has taken over the school cafeteria and introduced his McMealworm Lunch. It consists of a McMealworm Burger, Roasted Roaches and a Cricket Cola. He also is offering the Beetle Combo which includes a Beetleburger, Cocoon Cola and Fried Flies. Now you have a choice of menus!

Work the problems on another paper.   **Answer Space**

1.	You buy 2 McMealworm Lunches at $.95 each. You give Buggs a $5.00 bill. How much change do you get?	
2.	Buggs uses 1,040 mealworms to make 40 McMealworm Burgers. Each mealworm costs $.02. How much does it cost to make each burger?	
3.	Buggs bought 1,987 cockroaches. He bought 10 times as many mealworms. How many mealworms and cockroaches did he buy altogether?	
4.	One week, the cafeteria sold 497 McMealworm Lunches at $.95 each. That same week, it sold 469 Beetle Combos at $1.29 each. Which lunch brought in the most money? How much more?	
5.	700 orders of Fried Flies use 47 flies per order. 800 orders of Roasted Roaches use 39 roaches in each order. Which item uses more total insects? How many more?	
6.	Buggs makes $.13 profit on each McMealworm Lunch and $.19 on each Beetle Combo. How much total profit would he make if he sold 400 McMealworm Lunches and 500 Beetle Combos?	
7.	Your principal treated the student council to lunch. They ordered 5 McMealworm Lunches and 7 Beetle Combos. The principal had $13.90. Was this enough to pay for all the lunches?	
8.	Your teacher bought a McMealworm Lunch on Monday and Tuesday. On Wednesday, Thursday and Friday, she bought a Beetle Combo. How much less than $10.00 did she spend?	
9.	Your friend bought the McMealworm Lunch, which costs $.95, for 20 days. You bought the Beetle in a Box Combo, which costs $1.29, for 20 days. How much more did your lunch cost?	
10.	Each order of Beetle in a Box uses 27 beetles which cost $.02 each. How many beetles would be needed for 50 orders? What is their total cost?	

Shifty Sam's "Rip-Off" Record Shop

Name _____

Shifty Sam sells the latest rock releases along with some oldies that go clear back to when your teachers were teenagers. You have to keep a close eye on Sam, however, or you may get ripped off.

Work the problems on another paper.

Answer Space

1. The Ear Splitters' latest release, regularly $8.98, is on sale at 5 records for $46.95. How much more or less would you pay at the sale price for all 5 records?

2. The Funky Monkeys new record went fast. Sam made $4,540.90 on 455 copies. The correct price should be $7.99. How much did Sam charge for each record? How much extra did he charge?

3. Sam made $4.59 profit on each copy of the 323 records he sold by the Brainbangers. He is supposed to get only $3.29 profit on each one. How much extra did he make on the 323 records?

4. Sam sold 4,000 copies of "Pink Snow and Purple People" at $11.19 each. This was $1.77 more than he should charge. How much more did he earn than he should have earned?

5. The Phony Phreaky Phoners charged Sam $3.67 each for 298 records. He sold the records for $9.09 each. How much did he receive in total sales? How much profit did he make?

6. Your teacher wanted to buy some records by Hart N. Soule which regularly sell for $3.67 each. Sam offered to sell her a dozen records for $44.00. How much will she save by buying a dozen records?

7. You wanted 180 copies of Hits of the 1940's to use as Frisbees. Each record cost $.79. Sam gave you $47.80 in change from $200. How much did he cheat you?

8. Sam sold 7,000 copies of Golden Oldies for $3.99 each. He made a $2.00 profit on each record. How much money did he get for all 7,000 copies? How much profit did he earn?

9. Sam charged $1.79 more for each copy of the Dippers' new album than he was supposed to. His price was $7.89, and he sold 3,500 copies. How much extra money did he get?

10. Sam sold 4,328 copies of Country Classics at $4.99 each. His profit was $1.45 on each one. How much money did he get in all? How much profit did he earn?

IF8747 Math Topics

Smelly Belly Knows Your Nose

Name _____

Smelly Belly wants to capture the perfume market at your school. She has an exquisite nose for delicate scents and delightful fragrances which she bottles and sells to the students.

POLECAT

Work the problems on another paper.

Answer Space

1. Perfectly Putrid has become the scent everybody has to have. Smelly Belly sold 385 bottles at $7.99 each. How much money did she receive?

2. She made $533.61 on sales of 49 bottles of Essence of Skunk to the athletic crowd. What did she charge for each bottle?

3. Smelly earned $987.34 on Phew! and $1,278.43 on Whew! What were her total earnings for these two scents?

4. Her newest fragrance is He Skunk for young men. She sold 298 bottles in the first week at $6.39 each. How much did she earn?

5. Smelly Belly received $657.57 for sales of Skunk Leather and $1,765.01 for sales of Stinky Minky. How much more did she receive for Stinky Minky?

6. She sold 98 bottles of Skunk Musk at $11.85 each. How much money did she earn?

7. Smelly sold 68 bottles of Polecat Perfume for a total of $930.92. How much did she charge for each bottle?

8. The students raved over Bouquet of B.O. and spent $3,642.03 in one month on it. Each bottle sold for $9.87. How many bottles were sold?

9. El Stinko Bath Oil made a nice Christmas gift for a special friend. Smelly earned $736.77 on sales of 123 bottles of this item. What was the price of each bottle?

10. She sold $4,789.01 worth of Skunk Balm for tired muscles and $2,997.43 worth of Nose Toes. How much more did she earn on Skunk Balm?

Booming Business at Pat's Pets Aplenty

Name _____

Pat wants to put "A Pet in Every Home," so he is having a gigantic sale on all of his wonderful pets.

Work the problems on another paper.

Answer Space

1.	Pat has 18 rabbits which he is selling for $2.99 each. How much money will he earn if he sells all 18 rabbits?
2.	You bought a pet parrot for $2.39 and a myna bird for $8.67. What was your total cost?
3.	He is selling 12 goldfish for $.84. How much does he receive for each goldfish?
4.	Your teacher bought a ribbon snake for the classroom. It cost $4.79. How much change did she receive from a $20.00 bill?
5.	Pat is selling a pet python for $9.99. A pet monkey costs $13.45. What is the difference in their prices?
6.	Your principal bought 60 guppies for the school carnival for $23.40. How much did each guppy cost?
7.	Pat is selling hamsters for $1.41 each. How much will he receive for 40 hamsters?
8.	Pat sold 10 cocker spaniel puppies for $2.99 each. How much did he receive for all 10?
9.	Your teacher loves rodents. She buys a pair of mice for $2.39 and a pair of hamsters for $3.13. How much does it cost her altogether?
10.	Pat sold 19 chameleons for a total of $41.04. How much did he charge for each chameleon?

76

Shifty Sam's Sale

Name _____

Shifty Sam sells almost anything you would want to buy. Shifty is having a sale, and he says he's almost giving things away. But be careful. Compare his sale prices with his regular prices before you decide to buy.

SALE $58.00

BEARS ONLY $9.00

Work the problems on another paper.

Answer Space

1.	Sam usually sells a football-shaped pencil sharpener for $1.39 and a dozen pencils for $1.45. On sale, he is offering both for $2.89. How much money will you save or lose on this sale?
2.	The Brainbashers' newest hit record usually costs $7.99. Weird Wanda's top hit is regularly $8.79. Sam is selling both together for $16.89. How much money will you save or lose on this sale?
3.	Baseball wristbands regularly sell for $.98 each, and baseball caps are $2.87. Sam will sell them together for $3.50. How much money will you save on this sale?
4.	The regular price for a skateboard is $34.57, and for a pair of roller skates it is $45.99. Sam will sell you both items together for $89.95. How much will you save or lose at the sale price?
5.	Sam usually sells a ten-speed bike for $167.98 and a dirt bike for $155.89. How much will you save at the sale price offering both bikes for $323.85?
6.	The normal price for a fake beard is $2.39. A fake mustache is $1.99. Sam will sell both for $3.99 during the sale. How much will you save by buying both?
7.	High-top sneakers are usually $39.67 a pair. Low-cut sneakers sell for $19.98 a pair. Sam will sell you both pairs for $49.99. How much money do you save or lose on this sale?
8.	Sam's regular price for Silly Stickers is $1.78, while Stinky Stickers cost $1.98. How much will you save at the sale price of $3.75 for both?
9.	A football helmet usually sells for $33.99. A pair of football cleats sells for $37.88. Sam is offering both for $70.00. How much do you save or lose at the sale price?
10.	The regular price for a Rabbit Patch Doll is $7.99. Goofy Gus, the talking stuffed bear, sells for $24.99. Sam will sell both together for $33.50. How much will you save or lose at the sale price?

Something's Fishy at Pat's Pet Shop

Name _____

Pat has received a gigantic shipment of fish at his pet shop for his "Love A Fish Sale." Help him figure out how much money he could make.

Work the problems on another paper.

Answer Space

1.	Pat has 1,750 guppies which he sells at 10 for $1.00. How much money will he get if he sells all of them?	
2.	Pat has 324 black mollies which he sells at 6 for $3.25. How much could he make on the black mollies?	
3.	Pat has 648 swordtails which he sells at 12 for $1.00. How much will he get if he sells all of them?	
4.	He was sent 371 white cloud fish which are now on sale at 7 for $.99. How much will Pat make if he sells all of the white clouds?	
5.	He has 675 neons which sell at 25 for $2.00. How much could Pat make by selling all of the neons?	
6.	Pat has 1,281 comet goldfish which he sells at 21 for $4.99. How much will he make if he sells all of them?	
7.	Pat sells 25 angelfish for $3.00. How much will he get for 900 angelfish?	
8.	He has 253 tiger barbs which he sells at 11 for $1.99. How much will he get if he sells all of them?	
9.	Pat has 168 head-and-tail-light fish which he is selling at 3 for $2.99. How much will he make if he sells all of them?	
10.	He has 1,452 telescope goldfish which he is selling at 33 for $6.79. If he sells them all, how much money will he receive?	

Snails in a Pail

Name _____

Sly Me Slugg, world-famous French chef, has made his fast food business, **Snails in a Pail,** the most popular restaurant in the whole area. This is his menu:

Slime Soup $.49
Slugburgers $1.69
Chicken-Fried Snails $2.99
Slimy Slush $.89
Snailcream Shakes $1.49
Snailbits Salad $1.09

Work the problems on another paper.

Answer Space

1.	Sly Me Slugg sold 60 Slimy Slushes and 40 Snailcream Shakes on Friday. How much did he make on drinks that day?	
2.	Your principal treated 15 of his teachers to Slugburgers. How much change did he receive from $40.00?	
3.	Your teacher was so hungry that she bought an order of everything on the menu. How much change did she get from a $10.00 bill?	
4.	Sly Me Slugg sold $43.61 in Slime Soup orders on Wednesday and $38.22 in soup orders on Thursday. How many orders of Slime Soup did he sell in those 2 days?	
5.	You had a party at **Snails in a Pail** and ordered 9 Slugburgers, 3 Chicken-Fried Snails, 2 Snailbits Salads, 5 Snailcream Shakes and 10 Slimy Slushes. What was the total cost for the party?	
6.	In one week, Sly Me Slugg sold 200 Slugburgers and 79 Chicken-Fried Snail orders. How much money did he earn from these 2 items?	
7.	You ordered 10 Slugburgers, 10 Snailcream Shakes and 10 Slimy Slushes. What was your total cost?	
8.	On Friday, Sly Me earned $1,252. On Saturday, he earned $1,765. On Sunday, he earned $2,998. What was his average daily earnings for those 3 days?	
9.	Hye N. Skye treated his entire basketball team to dinner at **Snails in a Pail.** They ordered 8 Slime Soups, 12 Chicken-Fried Snails, 4 Slugburgers and 10 Slimy Slushes. What was the bill?	
10.	Sly Me Slugg sold $161.46 worth of Chicken-Fried Snails and $116.22 worth of Snailcream Shakes on a Saturday. How many orders of each item did he sell?	

Big Bucks for You!

Use with page 81.

Name _____

Your book, *The Secret Life of a Teenage Dracula*, earns you a nice bit of money in royalties. (A **royalty** is the publisher's payment to you as author of the book.) You need a checking account to keep the money in while you find ways to spend your new wealth.

Use the information on the next page and compute your payments, deposits and balance on the checkbook record below.

Problem Number	Transaction	Payment	Deposit	Balance
1	Deposit (Royalty Check)		$1000.00	$1000.00
1	Record Store			

Work the problems on another paper.   Skill: Balancing a checkbook   **Answer Space**

1. You receive your first royalty check for $1,000.00 and deposit it in your checking account. You go directly to the record store and spend $234.56 on new records. What is your balance?

2. You naturally treat all your friends to pizzas which costs you $47.76. You pay with a check. What is your balance now?

3. You decide to restock your wardrobe and buy $389.99 worth of new clothes. What is your balance?

4. Your next royalty check arrives, and you deposit $1,712.34. You also treat yourself to a new 15-speed bicycle which costs $667.09. What is your balance?

5. You buy your teacher some perfume for a present. You write a check for $37.89. What is your balance?

6. You need a tennis racket and some other sports equipment. The bill comes to $203.45. What is your new balance?

7. You treat your family to dinner at **Snails in a Pail** where the check comes to $56.17. What is your new balance?

8. You join a health club, and the first payment is $150.90. What is your new balance?

9. You deposit your latest royalty check which amounts to $4,451.01. What is your new balance?

10. To celebrate this good fortune, you take the entire school to a professional football game. The bill comes to $4,339.98. What is your new balance?

11. You need a good radio to boom out your favorite music. You spend $198.79 on a radio that is "state of the art." What is your new balance?

12. Your best friend borrows $500.00 from you. What is your balance?

13. You get a royalty check from your book for $456.78. What is your new balance?

14. You run up a large phone bill which comes to $793.55. What is your new balance?

Hairy Spiders and Mighty Mites

Name _____

Work the problems on another paper.

Answer Space

1. A male spitting spider is 4/16 in. long. A female is 3/8 in. long. How much longer is the female?	
2. A forest wolf spider is 1/2 in. long. A female rabid wolf spider is 3/4 in. long. What is the difference in their lengths?	
3. A male trapdoor spider is 11/12 in. long. A violin spider is 1/4 in. long. How much longer is the trapdoor spider?	
4. A female green lynx spider is 5/8 in. long. A male is 1/2 in. long. What is their total length?	
5. A male barn spider is 2/3 in. long. A female is 7/8 in. long. What is their total length?	
6. A male hammock spider is 1/4 in. long. A female is 1/3 in. long. What is their total length?	
7. A velvet mite is 1/8 in. long. A soft tick is 3/12 in. long. What is the difference in their lengths?	
8. A spider mite is only 1/32 in. long. A water mite is 1/8 in. long. How much longer is a water mite?	
9. A female garden spider is 3/4 in. long. A male is 6/12 in. long. How much longer is the female?	
10. A female bola spider is 1/2 in. long. A male bola is 1/12 in. long. What is the total?	

IF8747 Math Topics

Sam Sillicook's Secret Recipe!

Name _____

Sam Sillicook, world famous pizza maker, has just published his super secret recipe for The Tongue Blaster Pizza. This is the recipe:

1/4 cup of Tabasco sauce   3/8 cup of mustard

1/3 cup of red onions   2/7 cup of chili pepper

2/5 cup of horseradish   2/9 cup of garlic

1/6 cup of cayenne pepper

Serves 6 hungry people

Work the problems on another paper.

1.

Your teacher wants to make a smaller serving. She is going to make only 1/3 times as much. How much will she need of each ingredient?

_____ cup of Tabasco sauce

_____ cup of red onions

_____ cup of horseradish

_____ cup of cayenne pepper

_____ cup of mustard

_____ cup of chili pepper

_____ cup of garlic

2.

Your mother is going to serve this recipe to her bridge club. She needs only 1/2 of the recipe. How much of each ingredient will she need?

_____ cup of Tabasco sauce

_____ cup of red onions

_____ cup of horseradish

_____ cup of cayenne pepper

_____ cup of mustard

_____ cup of chili pepper

_____ cup of garlic

3.

The principal decides to bring this treat to the teachers' Christmas party. He is going to make 5/6 times as much as the recipe reads. How much of each ingredient will he need?

_____ cup of Tabasco sauce

_____ cup of red onions

_____ cup of horseradish

_____ cup of cayenne pepper

_____ cup of mustard

_____ cup of chili pepper

_____ cup of garlic

4.

You decide to make 1/4 as much of this recipe for your favorite teacher. How much will you need of each ingredient?

_____ cup of Tabasco sauce

_____ cup of red onions

_____ cup of horseradish

_____ cup of cayenne pepper

_____ cup of mustard

_____ cup of chili pepper

_____ cup of garlic

Eartha Wurm's New Pizzas

Name _____

Eartha Wurm believes that pizzas have become flat, dull, tasteless and boring. She has created new pizza toppings to put some zing back into your taste buds.

Work the problems on another paper.	**Answer Space**
1. Eartha Wurm wanted to cut 7 Red Hot Red Worm Pizzas into slices. Each slice would be 1/5 of a pizza. How many slices could she get from the 7 pizzas?	
2. Each slice of Spicy Caterpillar Pizza is 1/6 of a pizza. How many slices could Eartha get from 15 of these pizzas?	
3. Eartha gave away 2/7 of a Tasty Angleworm Pizza to each customer until all 12 of these pizzas were gone. How many customers received free pizza?	
4. Eartha Wurm made 10 Fiery Flatworm Pizzas. She cut them into 1/4 size pieces. How many pieces of Flatworm Pizza did she have?	
5. Every child under 7 feet tall was given 1/3 of a Chili Roundworm Pizza. Eartha gave away 40 of these pizzas. How many children received free pizza?	
6. Eartha's Wiggly Worm 'n Horseradish Pizza is so hot that she will sell only 2/9 of a pizza to each customer. How many customers can she serve with 16 of these pizzas?	
7. Each member of your softball team was treated to 3/7 of a Tangy Earthworm Pizza. It took 6 pizzas to treat all of you. How many members were on your team?	
8. The entire cast of your school play was rewarded with 3/5 of a Sweet and Sour Night Crawler Pizza. It took 18 pizzas. How many people took part in your school play?	
9. Eartha Wurm gave 4/9 of a pizza free to every person who came into her restaurant dressed like an earthworm. She gave away 4 pizzas. How many people came dressed up as earthworms?	
10. Your music teacher treated every member of the school chorus to 5/12 of a pizza. It took 20 pizzas. How many children were in the school chorus?	

Kookey's Cubic Cookie Cakes

Name _____

Professor Kook E. Kookey, inventor of the cubic cookie, has now created the ultimate dessert, the Cubic Cookie Cake, loaded with sweet things to make your taste buds tingle.

Work the problems on another paper.

Answer Space

1. Kook E. Kookey sold you 2/5 of his famous Cherry Berry Cubic Cookie Cake. Your friend bought 3/4 of a Cherry Berry. What was the sum?

2. Your principal is plum nuts over Professor Kookey's Plum Nuts Cubic Cookie Cake. He bought 6/7 of the cake. He gave 2/21 to his wife and ate the rest himself. How much did he eat?

3. The professor gave you 7/9 of a Jelly-Jammed Cubic Cookie Cake. He gave your best friend 5/6 of one of these cakes. How much more did your friend get?

4. Kook E. Kookey baked 24 Upside-Down Cubic Cookie Cakes. Your math teacher bought 5/8 of them for a class treat. How many cakes did he buy?

5. Your English teacher bought 32 Downside-Up Cubic Cookie Cakes. She divided them evenly among all of her students, giving each student 4/11 of a cake. How many students does she have?

6. "Slammin-Jammin" Mann ate 5/7 of a Plum Nuts Cake. "Boom Boom" Baker ate 7/11 of a Plum Nuts Cake. Who ate more cake? How much more?

7. Kook sold 5/12 of his 48 Stuffed Full of Stuff Cubic Cookie Cakes to Hye N. Skye. How many cakes did Hye N. Syke buy?

8. His brother Lowe N. Skye bought 6/7 of Professor Kookey's 84 Whipped Cream Dreams. How many did he buy?

9. You ate 7/12 of a Whipped Cream Dream for lunch and 1/8 of the same cake for dinner. How much did you eat altogether?

10. Kook had 4/5 of a Black 'n Blueberry Cubic Cookie Cake left. He cut it into 1/20-size pieces. How many pieces did he get?

Mr. M.T. Whole's Doughnut Shoppe

Skill: Solving problems with fractions and whole numbers
– mixed operations

Name _____

Mr. M.T. Whole bakes doughnuts that make your whole body quiver with anticipation. He is especially proud of his Jam-Crammed Jelly Doughnuts and his Creamy Delights.

Work the problems on another paper.

		Answer Space
1.	M.T. Whole used 15 ounces of jelly to make a batch of jelly doughnuts. Each doughnut used 1/4 ounce of jelly. How many doughnuts did he fill with the 15 ounces?	
2.	M.T. used 16 ounces of sugar for a batch of Whole's Holes. He used only 3/4 times as much sugar in his plain cake doughnuts. How much sugar did he use in his plain cakes?	
3.	He used 3/4 of a gallon of milk for a batch of Creamy Delights and 4/5 of a gallon of milk for a batch of Cupid's Custard Doughnuts. How much milk did he use in all?	
4.	A batch of Jam-Crammed Jelly Doughnuts required 7/8 of a gallon of jam. M.T. used 1/6 times as much jam in his regular jam doughnuts. How much jam did he use in the regular doughnuts?	
5.	Fudge-Filled Doughnuts use 5/7 of a pound of sugar. Dieters' Dream Doughnuts use 1/4 of a pound of sugar. How much more sugar is in a batch of Fudge-Filled Doughnuts?	
6.	His Whole's Holes each used 1/8 of an ounce of sprinkles. How many Holes could he cover with 9 ounces of sprinkles?	
7.	M.T.'s Double Twisted Twists used 1/9 of a pound of batter for each one. Each of his plain doughnuts used 3/4 times as much batter. How much batter was in each plain doughnut?	
8.	He gave you 10 doughnuts for being such a good customer. He gave your best friend 3/5 times as many doughnuts. How many doughnuts did your best friend receive?	
9.	M.T. Whole used 5/6 of a gallon of whipped cream for his Creamy Delights and 2/3 of a gallon of whipped cream for his Cupid's Custards. How much whipped cream did he use in all?	
10.	M.T. Whole's Double Twisted Twists used 3/4 of an ounce of sugar for each twist. How many twists were made with 60 ounces of sugar?	

Mean Monster Meets Molly Mugwumps

Name _____

It was love at first bite. They met at Sam Sillicook's Pizza Palace, and neither person had a dainty appetite. Figure out how much they ate.

Work the problems on another paper.

Answer Space

1. Mean Monster ate 2 1/3 pepperoni pizzas. Molly ate 1 1/2 pepperoni pizzas. What was their total?

2. Sam had 10 7/8 regular pizzas. They ate only 3 1/2 regular pizzas. How many regular pizzas did Sam have left?

3. Molly drank 2 5/6 cherry-lime colas. Mean Monster drank only 1 1/3 cherry-lime colas. How much more did Molly drink?

4. Molly sipped 5 1/2 strawberry shakes. Mean Monster sipped 4 1/3 shakes. How much did they sip altogether?

5. Mean Monster ate 6 7/10 chocolate chip cookies. Molly ate only 3 2/5 chocolate chip cookies. How many more cookies did Mean Monster eat?

6. Sam sold 6 7/8 Strawberry Pizza Tarts to this couple. Mean Monster ate 5 3/4 of them. How many did Molly get?

7. Molly loves Sam's Whipped Cream Pizza Desserts. She ate 4 1/3 of them. Mean Monster ate 2 1/5 of them. How many more desserts did Molly eat?

8. Mean Monster is allowed to eat only 2 1/2 pounds of food for dinner on his diet. He ate 6 5/8 pounds. How much more did he eat than his diet allowed?

9. Molly is allowed only 2 1/4 pounds of food for dinner on her diet. She pigged out and ate 5 9/10 pounds of food. How much more did she eat than her diet allowed?

10. Mean Monster gorged himself on 2 3/5 Whipped Cream Pizza Desserts. Molly devoured 3 1/10 of the same dessert. How much did they eat in all?

Smelly Belly's Perfume Parlor

Name _____

Smelly Belly is a skunk with a very refined sense of smell. She has started her own perfume business so that others can have an opportunity to enjoy all of her fragrances. Some of her favorite perfumes are Stinkpot, Stench and Fusty Musty.

Work the problems on another paper.

		Answer Space
1.	Smelly Belly sold 3 1/3 gallons of Stench on Monday. She sold 2 1/4 times as much Stench on Tuesday. How many gallons did she sell on Tuesday?	
2.	Smelly sold 8 1/3 gallons of Funky Skunky Bath Oil in a week. The next week, she sold 2 2/5 times as much. How many gallons were sold the second week?	
3.	Her Skunk-Scented Bath and Beauty Soap is so popular that she sold 5 1/4 cases one week and 3 3/7 times as much the next week. How many cases were sold the second week?	
4.	Smelly's brother Stinky Belly bought 6 bottles of Eau de Skunk for his girlfriend. Each bottle contained 4 1/3 ounces. How many ounces were in all 6 bottles?	
5.	He-Man Skunk Musk can be bought in a 1 1/2 ounce bottle. Smelly Belly sold 20 bottles. How many ounces were in all 20 bottles?	
6.	Smelly sold 7 1/3 cases of Phew in January. She sold only 9/11 as much in February. How many cases were sold in February?	
7.	Smelly's most popular scent is Putrid Polecat. Each bottle contains 2 1/9 ounces. How many ounces are contained in a case of 18 bottles?	
8.	Smelly Belly sold 7 1/2 cases of Stinkpot for Stinkers in December. The next month, she sold 3 3/5 times as much. How many cases were sold in January?	
9.	A bottle of White Stripe Cologne contains 2 5/6 ounces. Black Cat Cologne contains 1 1/5 times as much. How many ounces are in a bottle of Black Cat Cologne?	
10.	El Stinko Bath Powder contains 7 1/5 ounces of powder. Reek Bath Powder contains 2 2/9 times as much powder. How many ounces are in a box of Reek Bath Powder?	

Krab E. Krabby

Name _____

Krab E. Krabby likes to make unusual things, but he gets very cranky trying to figure out how much material he needs. Give him a hand so he won't be crabby.

Work the problems on another paper.

Answer Space

1.	Krab E. Krabby wants to make a paper clip jump rope 60 inches long. Each paper clip is 1 1/4 in. long. How many paper clips will he need?	
2.	Mr. Krabby wants to make a 39-inch-long belt by stringing string beans together. Each string bean is exactly 3 1/4 in. long. How many string beans will he need?	
3.	Krab E. Krabby hopes to make a 45-inch-high tower using dead batteries. Each battery is 2 1/2 in. tall. How many batteries will he need?	
4.	He is anxious to make a 9-inch-long wristband of seashells for his favorite teacher. He is going to use 1 1/8-inch-long seashells. How many will he need?	
5.	Krab would like to put a 180-inch border around his teacher's desk using pine cones that are 4 1/2 in. long. How many cones will he need?	
6.	Krabby wants to give his sister a 30-inch-long string of beads for her birthday. Each bead is 1 1/2 inches in diameter. How many beads will he need?	
7.	He is going to put together a 13-inch headband decorated with buttons that are 1 5/8 inches in diameter. How many buttons will he need?	
8.	He is going to glue together bottle caps that are 1 7/8 inch in diameter to make a school banner 150 inches long. How many bottle caps will he need?	
9.	Krab is gluing jumbo jellybeans end-to-end to create a jellybean necklace 20 inches long for his girlfriend. Each jellybean is 2 1/2 in. long. How many of them will he need?	
10.	Krabby wants to make an 81-inch border for the science counter using clam shells that are exactly 3 3/8 in. long. How many clam shells will he need?	

Mr. M.T. Whole Creates the Super Twist

Skill: Solving problems with mixed numbers (4 operations)

Name _____

Mr. M.T. Whole has invented a whole new kind of doughnut which he calls the Super Twist. It is filled with whipped cream, jammed with jelly and topped with powdered sugar.

Work the problems on another paper.

Answer Space

1. M.T. Whole uses 3 1/2 gallons of milk to make a batch of Whole Jelly Twists. He uses 1 3/4 gallons of milk for a batch of Plain Twists. What is the difference?

2. M.T. Whole needs 10 1/3 gallons of jam a week for his Super Jam-Filled Doughnut Twists. He needs only 4/5 as much jam for his Regular Jam Doughnuts. How much does he need for them?

3. Mr. Whole wants to make as many Super Twists as he can with 280 ounces of strawberry jam. Each twist uses 2 4/5 ounces of jam. How many Super Twists can he make?

4. M.T. is making a huge batch of Creamy Blackberry Twists which requires 198 5/6 ounces of flour. He is also using 134 7/8 ounces of flour for his Plain Twists. What is the total?

5. His Stuffed Strawberry Twists use 1 1/3 ounces of jam in each twist. How many twists can he fill with 124 ounces of jam?

6. M.T.'s Chock Full of Chocolate Twists require 3 5/7 ounces of chocolate for each one. How many ounces of chocolate are in 84 Chock Full of Chocolate Twists?

7. In one week, M.T. uses 114 1/2 gallons of milk and 99 7/9 gallons of cream. How much more milk does he use in a week?

8. M.T. uses 66 1/2 ounces of grape jelly for his Great Grape Twists. A batch of his Blueberry Twists requires 49 9/10 ounces of jelly. How many more ounces of grape jelly does he use?

9. Mr. M.T. Whole is especially proud of the Dreamy Creamy Twist, a scrumptious doughnut that uses 2 8/9 ounces of creamy filling. How many ounces of filling are in 84 Dreamy Creamy Twists?

10. M.T. Whole's Chock Full of Chocolate Twists each require 4 1/3 ounces of flour. How many ounces does he need for 180 of these doughnuts?

IF8747 Math Topics

McMealworms Introduce the Super Sac

Name _____

McMealworms wants your business. They have just introduced the Super Sac, a triple decker McMealworm Burger that comes with Roasted Roaches and a Cricket Cola.

Work the problems on another paper.

		Answer Space
1.	You buy a Super Sac for $3.79. How much change do you get from a $20.00 bill?	
2.	Your best friend buys a Super Sac for $3.79 and an extra order of Roasted Roaches for $.79. What is his total bill?	
3.	The largest cockroach you can find in your order of Roasted Roaches is 5.1 cm long. The shortest is 3.99 cm long. What is their total length?	
4.	Your mother spends $14.39 at McMealworms, and your sister spends another $4.99. What is their total cost?	
5.	The longest mealworm you can find in your Super Sac is 3.19 cm long. The shortest one is 1.7 cm. What is the difference in their lengths?	
6.	If you buy a triple decker burger, Roasted Roaches and a Cricket Cola separately, it costs $4.27. How much do you save by buying the Super Sac?	
7.	A regular McMealworm Burger costs $1.69. A triple decker costs $2.59. How much more is the triple decker?	
8.	You find one cockroach that weighs .321 grams and another that weighs .4 grams. What is their total weight?	
9.	Your friend finds a mealworm beetle that weighs .41 grams. The heaviest one you can find is .378 grams. How much heavier is your friend's beetle?	
10.	What is the difference in length between a 3.17 cm long mealworm and a 1.6 cm long mealworm?	

Kookey's Cubic Cookie Candy Bar

Name _____

Professor Kook E. Kookey has invented a cookie that is shaped like a child's alphabet block and tastes like a super sweet candy bar. He also has cubic cookie candy bars that are crammed with berries and chunks of chocolate.

Work the problems on another paper.

Answer Space

1.	Professor Kookey's Fudge-Filled Cubic Cookie Candy Bar has 3.7 ounces of fudge. How many ounces are in 35 bars?	
2.	Kook E. Kookey's Chock Full of Chocolate Cookie Candy Bar has 5.3 ounces of chocolate. How many ounces are in 68 bars?	
3.	Kook's Cubic Munchy Crunchies use 6.78 ounces of peanuts in each one. How many ounces are there in .25 of a bar?	
4.	Kookey's Crunchies also use 5.34 ounces of maple sugar. How much maple sugar is in .25 of a bar?	
5.	His Chunky Chocolate Cubic Cookie Candy Bars have 12.306 ounces of chocolate in each bar. How many ounces are in 3.5 bars?	
6.	Kookey needs 7.5 ounces of cream for each Stuffed Strawberry and Cream Bar. How many ounces does he use for 30.5 bars?	
7.	Professor Kookey's Stuffed Strawberry and Cream Bars each need 11.504 ounces of berries. How many ounces of berries are in 40 bars?	
8.	Kook E.'s Caramel Raspberry Cubic Cookie Candy Bars use 4.67 ounces of caramel in each bar. How many ounces of caramel are in .33 of a bar?	
9.	Professor Kookey uses 5.6 ounces of blueberries for his Blueberry and Banana Bars. How many ounces does he need for 200 bars?	
10.	Kook E. Kookey's Lemondrop Lollipop Cubic Cookie Candy Bars each have 2.013 ounces of lemon flavoring. How many ounces are needed for 28 bars?	

You and Major League Baseball

Name _____

You have won a national contest sponsored by Olog's Groaty Oaties. The prize is a chance for you to play in the majors. All you have to do is bat over .300 against the majority of the major leaguers.

Reminder: To find your batting average divide the number of "at bats" into the number of "hits." Add a decimal point and 3 zeroes to the number of hits. ($4.000 \div 10 = .400$)

Work the problems on another paper.

		Answer Space
1.	You got 4 hits in 10 at bats against Dizzy Dolan. What was your batting average against Dizzy?	
2.	You faced Herman "The Tank" Sherman and belted out 16 hits in 20 trips to the plate. What was your average against Herman?	
3.	Against the famous pitcher, "Moonbeam" Malone, you smacked 7 hits in 14 trips to the plate. What was your batting average against Moonbeam?	
4.	You smashed 13 hits in 20 at bats against "Bullets" Bascom. What was your batting average against Bullets?	
5.	You faced the fireballing pitcher called Lefty Writey and banged out 9 hits in 12 times at bat. What was your batting average against Lefty?	
6.	You crushed 5 hits in 8 at bats against "Piano Legs" Jones. What was your batting average against Jones?	
7.	"Lightning" Bill Smith gave you a hard time, and you got only 2 hits in 10 at bats. What was your average against Bill?	
8.	You crunched "Knuckles" McBain for 12 hits in 16 at bats. What was your batting average?	
9.	You smashed 17 hits in 20 at bats against Victor "The Vulture" Rollins. What was your batting average against Rollins?	
10.	Altogether you belted out 114 hits in 175 at bats. What was your overall batting average?	

Creepy Crawly Critters

Name _____

Work the problems on another paper.

Answer Space

1. A female black widow spider is 9 mm long. An Eastern diamondback rattlesnake is 250 times as long. How long is the snake?	
2. A male black cockroach is 2.5 cm long. A female is 3.499 cm long. What is the length of both together?	
3. A baby sidewinder is 20 cm long. An adult is 4.1 times as long. How long is the adult?	
4. A gila monster is 60.9 cm long. A copperhead snake is 134.6 cm long. How much longer is the snake?	
5. An American alligator is 5.84 m long. An American crocodile is 4.6 m long. What is the difference?	
6. A glass lizard is 106.699 cm long. A Southern alligator lizard is 42.8 cm long. What is the difference?	
7. A male grass spider is 1.5 cm long. A female is 1.334 times as long. How long is the female?	
8. A male rabid wolf spider is 1.3 cm long. A female is 1.611 times as long. How long is the female?	
9. A yellow-bellied water snake is 157.50 cm long. You could lay 225 bed bugs in a line that long. How long is each bed bug?	
10. A green water snake is 185.6 cm long. You could lay 32 elephant stag beetles in a line that long. How long is a stag beetle?	

The N.B.A. Wants You

Name _____

You have just been named "The Young Basketball Player of the Year." Your reward is a chance to go one-on-one against the superstars of the N.B.A.

Instructions: Compute your shooting percentage and round it off to the nearest whole percent.

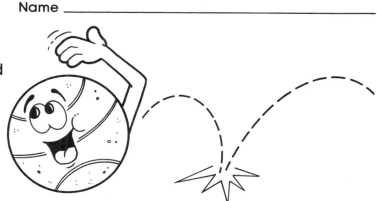

Work the problems on another paper.	Answer Space
1. You hit 13 out of 20 against Sam "Bamm-Bamm" Smith. What was your shooting percentage?	
2. "Bamm-Bamm" nailed only 3 shots out of 20 against you. What percentage did he shoot?	
3. Against Hye N. Skye you hit 15 baskets in 25 attempts. What was your percentage?	
4. Hye N. Skye made only 8 out of 25 shots against you. What was his percentage?	
5. You sank 7 of 14 shots against James "Slick Shot" Jones. What was your shooting percentage?	
6. "Slick" hit 6 out of 14 shots against you. What did he shoot?	
7. You hit 9 out of 12 shots against "Slammin'-Jammin' " Mann. What was your shooting percentage?	
8. "Slammin'-Jammin' " sank only 2 of 12 shots while you guarded him. What did he shoot?	
9. You hit 15 of 22 shots against "Dunkin" Dolan. What was your shooting percentage?	
10. "Dunkin" iced only 4 of 22 against you. What did he shoot?	

The National Football League Wants You!

Name _____

You were so spectacular in your last school football game that every team in the N.F.L. wanted to draft you as their number 1 quarterback. You ended up with a new team that really needed your help, the **Oki Doki Outlaws.**

Compute your passing percentage against these teams to the nearest whole percent.

Work the problems on another paper.	**Answer Space**
1. You completed 25 out of 30 passes against the Nevada Gamblers led by "Lucky Ducky" Tucky. What was your percentage of completions?	
2. "Brainbasher" Brown and the Boston Bobcats were no match for you. You completed 16 of 24 passes. What was your passing percentage?	
3. You faced the Kansas Coyotes led by Doc "The Scalpel" Jones and still completed 11 out of 16 attempts. What was your percentage of completions?	
4. The Missouri Maulers really tried to maul you, but you still connected for 17 passes out of 25 attempts. What was your completion percentage?	
5. The Arizona Alleycats, led by linebacker "All Bad" Larry Badd, were no match for your perfect passes. You completed 33 out of 36 attempts. What was your passing percentage?	
6. The Texas Tornadoes, led by linebacker "Bonemuncher" Bolanger, tried to contain you, but you still completed 28 out of 40 passes. What was your percentage?	
7. The Virginia Vigilantes, with their great linebacker, "The Steel Wheel" Peale, gave you some trouble. You completed 11 out of 34 attempts. What was your passing percentage?	
8. Ivan "The Intimidator" Evans led the Florida Flyers against you. You were unimpressed and hit 37 of 42 passes. What was your percentage of completions?	
9. Clarence "Clank" Clunker gave you a hard time, and you hit only 7 of 23 against the Utah Utes. What was your percentage of completions?	
10. During the season, you completed 234 passes out of 298 attempts. What was your passing percentage for the season?	

Time Out for Molly Mugwumps

Name _____

Molly Mugwumps is disorganized. Her room looks like it was designed by a hurricane. Her closet is stuffed full of stuff and her locker is a disaster. She especially needs help managing her time.

Work the problems on another paper.

Answer Space

1. Molly Mugwumps woke up at 6:50 a.m. It took her 27 minutes to shower and dress. When did she finish?

2. Molly arrived at school at 9:08 a.m. It took her 47 minutes to get there. When did she start out?

3. Molly started breakfast at 7:45 a.m. and finished at 8:25 a.m. How long did it take?

4. Molly took 49 minutes to eat lunch which she finished at 12:22 p.m. When did she start?

5. She spent 2 hours and 47 minutes playing football. She finished at 7:10 p.m. When did she begin?

6. Molly spent 2 hours and 17 minutes watching cartoons. She started at 3:45 p.m. When did she stop?

7. She spent 3 hours and 49 minutes cleaning her room on Saturday. She started at 10:55 a.m. When did she finish?

8. Molly spent 2 hours and 13 minutes on the phone giggling with her girlfriend. She dialed at 6:53 p.m. When did she hang up?

9. She wanted to set the school record for the longest phone call. She dialed at 4:49 p.m. and hung up 13 hours and 59 minutes later. What time was it?

10. Molly set the class record for the longest time chewing the same piece of gum. She started at 9:22 a.m. and swallowed it at 2:09 p.m. How long did she chew?

Mean Monster Puts a Lock on Wrestling

Name _____

Mean Monster, a great defensive back in football, decided to take on all the top wrestlers in order to keep in shape during the off-season. He weighed 569 lbs. 7 oz. and stood 7 ft. 3 in. tall.
(Remember: 1 lb. = 16 oz.   1 ft. = 12 in.)

Work the problems on another paper.	Answer Space
1. Mean Monster's first bout was with Harry "The Hammer" Brown who weighed 397 lbs. 4 ounces. How much more did Mean Monster weigh?	
2. He did so well in his first round that he faced Marvelous Marvin Morton in the next event. Marvelous Marvin stood 6 ft. 9 in. tall. How much taller was Mean Monster?	
3. Awesome Albert Alston was 167 lbs. 11 oz. lighter than Mean Monster. What did Awesome Albert weigh?	
4. Irwin "The Icebox" weighed 478 lbs. 14 oz. He and Mean Monster stood together on the scale. What did it read?	
5. Dazzling Doug Dugan ate 146 oz. of meat before the match. Mean Monster ate 5 lbs. 9 oz. of meat. How much meat did they eat altogether?	
6. Si "Stilts" Stone stood 8 ft. 1 in. tall. How much shorter was Mean Monster?	
7. Dreadful Dan "The Mighty Man" weighed 777 lbs. 7 oz. What was his weight in ounces?	
8. Ivan the Incredible ate an 18 lb. 8 oz. meal before his bout. Mean Monster had only 188 oz. of food before the match. How much more did Ivan eat?	
9. Melvin the Magnificent was a dainty 478 lbs. 15 oz. He stood with Mean Monster and Dreadful Dan on the same scale. What was their total weight?	
10. Mean Monster's brother Itty Bitty Monster weighed 134 lbs. 15 oz. less than his big brother. What did Itty Bitty weigh?	

Molly Cleans Up the School . . . Sort Of

Name _____

Molly Mugwumps has a problem keeping her things in order. Even her own desk is a jumbled-up mess! Nevertheless, she has decided to tidy up the school.

Key Facts: Perimeter = (length + width) x 2
Area = length x width
Volume = length x width x height

Work the problems on another paper.   **Answer Space**

1.	Molly Mugwumps wants to string a "Welcome" banner all the way around the school which is 150 feet long and 50 feet wide. How long will the banner have to be?	
2.	Molly believes that the nurse's office needs a black wall to go with all that white. The wall is 12 ft. high and 11 ft. wide. How many square feet of black wallpaper will she need?	
3.	Molly knows that the principal loves to play golf, so she wants to fill her office with golf balls. The office is 12 ft. high, 10 ft. wide and 11 ft. long. How many cubic feet of golf balls will she need?	
4.	Molly wants to string a border of lavender stones all the way around the playground which is 120 ft. long and 70 ft. wide. What is the perimeter of the playground?	
5.	Molly loves her teacher and wants to cover her classroom door with purple and green striped wallpaper. The door is 8 ft. high and 4 1/2 ft. wide. How many sq. ft. of wallpaper will she need?	
6.	Molly wants to give a new sandbox filled with pink sand to her former kindergarten teacher. The box is 5 ft. wide, 4 ft. long and 2.5 ft. high. How many cubic feet of sand does she need?	
7.	Molly wants to spruce up the top of her teacher's desk with a pink and orange polka-dotted blotter. The desk is 6 ft. long and 3.4 ft. wide. What is the area of the blotter she will need?	
8.	Her teacher loves marbles, and Molly wants to fill her whole closet at school with them. The closet is 8 ft. high, 2 ft. wide and 3 ft. long. How many cubic feet of marbles will Molly need?	
9.	Molly wants to put a pretty border of crepe paper all the way around the school cafeteria which is 27 ft. wide and 42 ft. long. How long will the crepe paper border be?	
10.	Molly helps the third grade teacher fill up a planter with dirt for the class garden. The planter is 1 1/2 ft. high, 2 1/2 ft. wide and 3 ft. long. How many cubic feet of dirt does she need?	

It's for the Birds

Name _____

Key Facts:
1 ft. = 12 in.
1 yd. = 3 ft. = 36 in.

Work the problems on another paper.

Answer Space

1. The black vulture has a wingspan of 60 inches. How many feet is its wingspan?

2. A gray hawk has a 3-foot wingspan. How many inches is that?

3. The turkey vulture has a 72-inch wingspan. How many yards is that?

4. A red-shouldered hawk has a 4-foot wingspan. How many inches can he spread his wings?

5. A sparrow hawk has a 24-inch wingspan. How many feet can its wings spread out?

6. A California condor has a 114-inch wingspan. How many feet is that? How many inches are left over?

7. The golden eagle has a wingspan of 7 ft. 8 in. How many inches is his wingspan?

8. The bald eagle has a 96-inch wingspan. What is his wingspan in feet?

9. A red-shouldered hawk is 2 feet long. How long is that in inches?

10. The red-tailed hawk has a 54-inch wingspan. How many feet is that? How many inches are left over?

Metric Measurement: The Bear Facts

Name _____

Key Facts:
1 meter = 100 centimeters = 1000 millimeters
1 centimeter = 10 millimeters

Work the problems on another paper.   **Answer Space**

1.	A black bear has a tail 190 mm long. How many cm is that?	
2.	The hind foot of a grizzly bear is 26 cm long. How many mm is that?	
3.	The claws of a grizzly bear are 10 cm long. How many mm is that?	
4.	A polar bear is 300 cm long. How many meters is that?	
5.	The grizzly bear is 130 cm tall. How tall is that in meters?	
6.	The tail of a polar bear is 130 mm long. How many cm is that?	
7.	A brown bear is 200 cm long. How many meters is that?	
8.	The black bear is 100 cm tall. How many meters tall is that?	
9.	A brown bear has a tail that is 70 mm long. How many cm is that?	
10.	The black bear is 188 cm long. How many mm long is the black bear?	

Leapin' Lizards

Name _____

Key Facts:

1 meter = 100 centimeters = 1000 millimeters
10 millimeters = 1 centimeter

Work the problems on another paper.   **Answer Space**

| 1. | A desert iguana is 40.6 cm long. How many mm is this? | |

| 2. | A gila monster is 61 cm long. How many meters is this? | |

| 3. | A jungle runner is 63.5 cm long. A gila whiptail is 30.6 cm long. What is the difference in their lengths? | |

| 4. | A racerunner is 26.7 cm long. How much less than a meter is this? | |

| 5. | A worm lizard is 40.6 cm long. How many cm less than a meter is this? | |

| 6. | A ruin lizard is 25 cm long. A green lizard is 13.7 cm longer than a ruin lizard. How long is the green lizard? | |

| 7. | A leopard lizard is 38.4 cm long. A common iguana is 200 cm long. How much longer is the iguana? | |

| 8. | A common iguana is 200 cm long. How many meters is this? | |

| 9. | A collard lizard is 35.6 cm long. How many mm is this? | |

| 10. | A curly-tailed lizard is 26.6 cm long. A short-tailed lizard is 14.9 cm long. What is the difference in their lengths? | |

Answer Key

Page 1

Addition of Time
Skill: addition of time with regrouping

Name _____

60 seconds	= 1 minute (min)	7 days	= 1 week (wk)
60 minutes	= 1 hour (h)	4 weeks	= 1 month (mo)
24 hours	= 1 day (d)	12 months or 52 weeks	= 1 year (y)

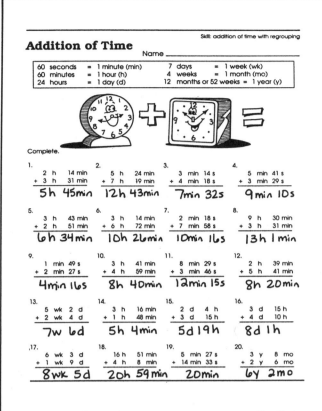

Complete.

1.
2 h 14 min
+ 3 h 31 min
5h 45min

2.
5 h 24 min
+ 7 h 19 min
12h 43min

3.
3 min 14 s
+ 4 min 18 s
7min 32s

4.
5 min 41 s
+ 3 min 29 s
9min 10s

5.
3 h 43 min
+ 2 h 51 min
6h 34min

6.
3 h 14 min
+ 6 h 72 min
10h 26min

7.
2 min 18 s
+ 7 min 58 s
10min 16s

8.
9 h 30 min
+ 3 h 31 min
13h 1min

9.
1 min 49 s
+ 2 min 27 s
4min 16s

10.
3 h 41 min
+ 4 h 59 min
8h 40min

11.
8 h 29 min
+ 3 h 46 min
12min 15s

12.
2 h 39 min
+ 5 h 41 min
8h 20min

13.
5 wk 2 d
+ 2 wk 4 d
7w 6d

14.
3 h 16 min
+ 1 h 48 min
5h 4min

15.
2 d 4 h
+ 3 d 15 h
5d 19h

16.
3 d 15 h
+ 4 d 10 h
8d 1h

17.
6 wk 3 d
+ 1 wk 9 d
8wk 5d

18.
16 h 51 min
+ 4 h 8 min
20h 59min

19.
5 min 27 s
+ 14 min 33 s
20min

20.
3 y 8 mo
+ 2 y 6 mo
6y 2mo

Page 1

Page 2

Subtraction of Time
Skill: subtraction of time with regrouping

Name _____

60 seconds	= 1 minute (min)	7 days	= 1 week (wk)
60 minutes	= 1 hour (h)	4 weeks	= 1 month (mo)
24 hours	= 1 day (d)	12 months or 52 weeks	= 1 year (y)

Complete.

1.
7 min 42 s
− 3 min 29 s
4min 13s

2.
5 h 49 min
− 2 h 34 min
3h 15min

3.
8 h 24 min
− 5 h 19 min
3h 5min

4.
4 min 47 s
− 3 min 28 s
1min 19s

5.
8 h 14 min
− 3 h 25 min
4h 49min

6.
7 h 29 min
− 2 h 38 min
4h 51min

7.
9 min 23 s
− 8 min 51 s
32s

8.
4 min 21 s
− 2 min 53 s
1min 28s

9.
12 min 19 s
− 8 min 42 s
3min 37s

10.
5 h 14 min
− 3 h 29 min
1h 45min

11.
16 min 42 s
− 8 min 25 s
8min 17s

12.
3 h 12 min
− 1 h 46 min
1h 26min

13.
5 d 9 h
− 2 d 10 h
2d 23h

14.
3 wk 4 d
− 1 wk 5 d
1wk 6d

15.
16 d 14 h
− 9 d 7 h
7d 7h

16.
6 y 4 mo
− 3 y 6 mo
2y 10mo

17.
5 min 21 s
− 2 min 22 s
2min 59s

18.
8 d 7 h
− 5 d 21 h
2d 10h

19.
5 wk 3 d
− 2 wk 6 d
2wk 4d

20.
13 h 14 min
− 7 h 48 min
5h 26min

21.
8 y 9 mo
− 2 y 10 mo
5y 11mo

22.
4 d 13 h
− 1 d 17 h
2d 20h

23.
21 h 10 min
− 8 h 54 min
12h 16min

24.
4 min 32 s
− 2 min 47 s
1min 45s

Page 2

Page 3

Different Ways of Telling Time
Skill: telling time two different ways

Name _____

Complete.

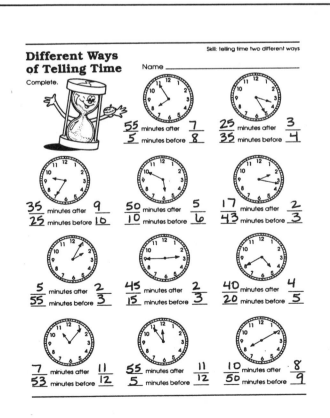

55 minutes after **7**
5 minutes before **8**

25 minutes after **3**
35 minutes before **4**

35 minutes after **9**
25 minutes before **10**

50 minutes after **5**
10 minutes before **6**

17 minutes after **2**
43 minutes before **3**

5 minutes after **2**
55 minutes before **3**

45 minutes after **2**
15 minutes before **3**

40 minutes after **4**
20 minutes before **5**

7 minutes after **11**
53 minutes before **12**

55 minutes after **11**
5 minutes before **12**

10 minutes after **8**
50 minutes before **9**

Page 3

Page 4

Time Conversion – I
Skill: conversion of time

Name _____

60 seconds	= 1 minute (min)	7 days	= 1 week (wk)
60 minutes	= 1 hour (h)	4 weeks	= 1 month (mo)
24 hours	= 1 day (d)	12 months or 52 weeks	= 1 year (y)

Complete.

1. 3 h = **180** min
2. 4 d = **96** h
3. 2 h = **120** min
4. 5 min = **300** s
5. 6 min = **360** s
6. 8 h = **480** min
7. 2 d = **48** h
8. 5 h = **300** min
9. 5 d = **120** h
10. 14 min = **840** s
11. 240 min = **4** h
12. 7 d = **168** h
13. 96 h = **4** d
14. 300 s = **5** min
15. 8 min = **480** s
16. $\frac{1}{6}$ d = **4** h
17. 9 h = **540** min
18. 180 min = **3** h
19. $\frac{1}{3}$ min = **20** s
20. 3 d = **72** h
21. 12 h = **720** min
22. 8 d = **192** h
23. 120 h = **5** d
24. 540 s = **9** min

Page 4

Answer Key

Time Conversion – II

Name _____

60 seconds	= 1 minute (min)	7 days	= 1 week (wk)
60 minutes	= 1 hour (h)	4 weeks	= 1 month (mo)
24 hours	= 1 day (d)	12 months or 52 weeks	= 1 year (y)

Complete.

1. 50 h = **2** d **2** h
2. 72 s = **1** min **12** s
3. 12 min 12 s = **732** s
4. 9 d = **1** wk **2** d
5. 2 d 6 hr = **54** h
6. 26 h = **1** d **2** h
7. 129 s = **2** min **9** s
8. 37 d = **5** wk **2** d
9. 189 min = **3** h **9** min
10. 4 d 4 hr = **100** h
11. 53 d = **7** wk **4** d
12. 78 h = **3** d **6** h
13. 5 min 14 s = **314** s
14. 484 min = **8** h **4** min
15. 6 wk 2 d = **44** d
16. 65 d = **9** wk **2** d
17. 369 s = **6** min **9** s
18. 2 wk 6 d = **20** d
19. 3 mo 2 wk = **14** wk
20. 55 wk = **1** y **3** wk
21. 16 mo = **1** y **4** mo
22. 88 d = **12** wk **4** d
23. 50 d = **7** wk **1** d
24. 39 wk = **9** mo **3** wk

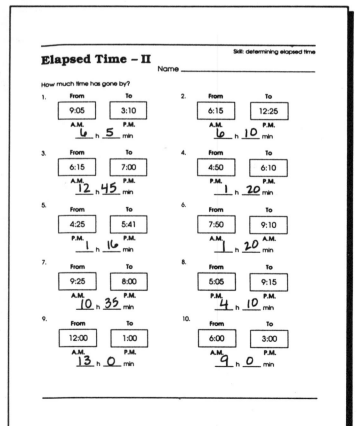

Elapsed Time – I

Name _____

How much time has gone by?

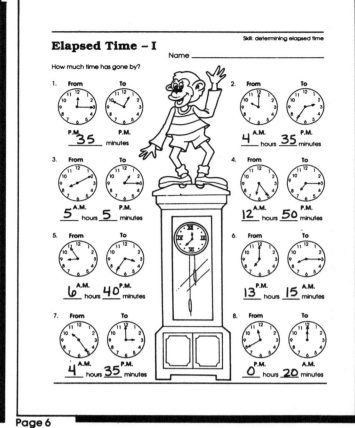

1. From P.M. To P.M. — **35** minutes
2. From A.M. To P.M. — **4** hours **35** minutes
3. From A.M. To P.M. — **5** hours **5** minutes
4. From A.M. To P.M. — **12** hours **50** minutes
5. From A.M. To P.M. — **6** hours **40** minutes
6. From P.M. To A.M. — **13** hours **15** minutes
7. From A.M. To P.M. — **4** hours **35** minutes
8. From P.M. To A.M. — **0** hours **20** minutes

Elapsed Time – II

Name _____

How much time has gone by?

1. From 9:05 A.M. To 3:10 P.M. — **6** h **5** min
2. From 6:15 A.M. To 12:25 P.M. — **6** h **10** min
3. From 6:15 A.M. To 7:00 P.M. — **12** h **45** min
4. From 4:50 P.M. To 6:10 P.M. — **1** h **20** min
5. From 4:25 P.M. To 5:41 P.M. — **1** h **16** min
6. From 7:50 A.M. To 9:10 A.M. — **1** h **20** min
7. From 9:25 A.M. To 8:00 P.M. — **10** h **35** min
8. From 5:05 P.M. To 9:15 P.M. — **4** h **10** min
9. From 12:00 A.M. To 1:00 P.M. — **13** h **0** min
10. From 6:00 A.M. To 3:00 P.M. — **9** h **0** min

Addition of Elapsed Time

Name _____

Figure the elapsed time.

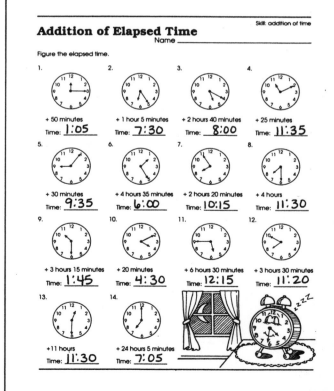

1. + 50 minutes — Time: **1:05**
2. + 1 hour 5 minutes — Time: **7:30**
3. + 2 hours 40 minutes — Time: **8:00**
4. + 25 minutes — Time: **11:35**
5. + 30 minutes — Time: **9:35**
6. + 4 hours 35 minutes — Time: **6:00**
7. + 2 hours 20 minutes — Time: **10:15**
8. + 4 hours — Time: **11:30**
9. + 3 hours 15 minutes — Time: **1:45**
10. + 20 minutes — Time: **4:30**
11. + 6 hours 30 minutes — Time: **12:15**
12. + 3 hours 30 minutes — Time: **11:20**
13. + 11 hours — Time: **11:30**
14. + 24 hours 5 minutes — Time: **7:05**

IF8747 Math Topics

Answer Key

More Addition of Time
Name _____
Skill: addition of time

Determine the sum total.

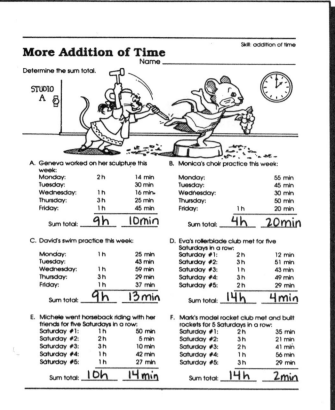

STUDIO A

A. Geneva worked on her sculpture this week:

Monday:	2h	14 min
Tuesday:		30 min
Wednesday:	1h	16 min
Thursday:	3h	25 min
Friday:	1h	45 min

Sum total: **9h 10min**

B. Monica's choir practice this week:

Monday:		55 min
Tuesday:		45 min
Wednesday:		30 min
Thursday:		50 min
Friday:	1h	20 min

Sum total: **4h 20min**

C. David's swim practice this week:

Monday:	1h	25 min
Tuesday:	1h	43 min
Wednesday:	1h	59 min
Thursday:	3h	29 min
Friday:	1h	37 min

Sum total: **9h 13min**

D. Eva's rollerblade club met for five Saturdays in a row:

Saturday #1:	2h	12 min
Saturday #2:	3h	51 min
Saturday #3:	1h	43 min
Saturday #4:	3h	49 min
Saturday #5:	2h	29 min

Sum total: **14h 4min**

E. Michele went horseback riding with her friends for five Saturdays in a row:

Saturday #1:	1h	50 min
Saturday #2:	2h	5 min
Saturday #3:	3h	10 min
Saturday #4:	1h	42 min
Saturday #5:	1h	27 min

Sum total: **10h 14min**

F. Mark's model rocket club met and built rockets for 5 Saturdays in a row:

Saturday #1:	2h	35 min
Saturday #2:	3h	21 min
Saturday #3:	2h	41 min
Saturday #4:	1h	56 min
Saturday #5:	3h	29 min

Sum total: **14h 2min**

Page 9

More Elapsed Time
Name _____
Skill: estimating future time and elapsed time

Complete.

	Time Now	Add this Elapsed Time	Future Time (Include Day and Time)
1.	Monday, 9:00 a.m.	2 days, 4 hours	W 1:00 p.m.
2.	Saturday, 4:00 p.m.	3 days, 5 hours, 32 minutes	Tu 9:32 p.m.
3.	Tuesday, 6:00 a.m.	6 days, 7 hours, 45 minutes	M 1:45 p.m.
4.	Sunday, 1:00 p.m.	1 day, 9 hours, 56 minutes	M 10:56 p.m.
5.	Thursday, 2:45 p.m.	5 days, 2 hours, 45 minutes	Tu 5:30 p.m.
6.	Wednesday, 4:00 a.m.	8 days, 12 hours, 29 minutes	Th 4:29 p.m.
7.	Monday, 7:00 a.m.	14 days, 7 hours, 39 minutes	M 2:39 p.m.
8.	Friday, 7:00 p.m.	2 days, 3 advanced time zones	Su 10:00 p.m.
9.	Monday, 5:00 p.m.	4 days, 25 hours	Sa 6:00 p.m.
10.	Saturday, 12:00 a.m.	6 days, 13 hours, 1 minute	F 1:01 p.m.
11.	Tuesday, 5:00 p.m.	12 days, 14 hours, 23 minutes	M 7:23 a.m.
12.	Sunday, 2:00 a.m.	3 days, 26 hours	Th 4:00 a.m.
13.	Monday, 1:00 p.m.	2 weeks, 4 days, 35 minutes	F 1:35 p.m.
14.	Saturday, 6:00 a.m.	74 hours	Tu 8:00 a.m.
15.	Sunday, 8:00 p.m.	21 days, 2 hours	Su 10:00 a.m.
16.	Wednesday, 4:00 a.m.	15 days, 12 hours, 45 minutes	Th 4:45 p.m.
17.	Friday, 3:00 p.m.	5 days, 3 hours, 128 minutes	W 8:08 p.m.
18.	Thursday, 6:00 p.m.	3 days, 4 earlier time zones	Su 2:00 p.m.

Complete. Give the elapsed time in days and hours.

1.	Monday, 4:00 a.m. to Wednesday, 5:00 a.m.	2d 1h
2.	Wednesday, 12:00 p.m. to Saturday, 2:00 p.m.	3d 2h
3.	Friday, 5:00 p.m. to Sunday, 4:00 p.m.	2d 11h
4.	Thursday, 7:00 p.m. to Friday, 9:00 a.m.	14h
5.	Saturday, 6:00 p.m. to Monday, 5:00 a.m.	1d 11h
6.	Tuesday, 3:00 p.m. to Friday, 6:00 p.m.	3d 3h
7.	Saturday, 8:00 p.m. to Sunday, 3:00 a.m.	7h
8.	Monday, 4:00 p.m. to Wednesday, 8:00 a.m.	1d 16h

Page 10

Bar Graphs
Name _____
Skill: working with bar graphs

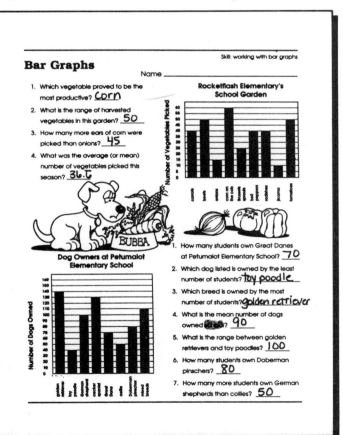

1. Which vegetable proved to be the most productive? **Corn**
2. What is the range of harvested vegetables in this garden? **50**
3. How many more ears of corn were picked than onions? **45**
4. What was the average (or mean) number of vegetables picked this season? **36.6**

Rocketflash Elementary's School Garden

Dog Owners at Petumalot Elementary School

BUBBA

1. How many students own Great Danes at Petumalot Elementary School? **70**
2. Which dog listed is owned by the least number of students? **toy poodle**
3. Which breed is owned by the most number of students? **golden retriever**
4. What is the mean number of dogs owned? **90**
5. What is the range between golden retrievers and toy poodles? **100**
6. How many students own Doberman pinschers? **80**
7. How many more students own German shepherds than collies? **50**

Page 11

Double Bar Graphs – I
Name _____
Skill: working with double bar graphs

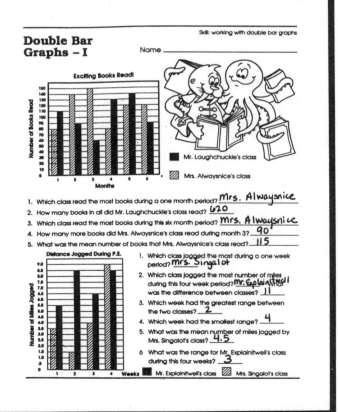

Exciting Books Read!

■ Mr. Laughchuckle's class
▨ Mrs. Alwaysnice's class

1. Which class read the most books during a one month period? **Mrs. Alwaysnice**
2. How many books in all did Mr. Laughchuckle's class read? **620**
3. Which class read the most books during this six month period? **Mrs. Alwaysnice**
4. How many more books did Mrs. Alwaysnice's class read during month 3? **90**
5. What was the mean number of books that Mrs. Alwaysnice's class read? **115**

Distance Jogged During P.E.

1. Which class jogged the most during a one week period? **Mrs. Singalot**
2. Which class jogged the most number of miles during this four week period? **Mr. Explainitwell** What was the difference between classes? **11**
3. Which week had the greatest range between the two classes? **2**
4. Which week had the smallest range? **4**
5. What was the mean number of miles jogged by Mrs. Singalot's class? **4.5**
6. What was the range for Mr. Explainitwell's class during this four weeks? **3**

■ Mr. Explainitwell's class ▨ Mrs. Singalot's class

Page 12

Answer Key

Page 13

Double Bar Graphs – II

Skill: working with double bar graphs

Name _____

Horseback Riders

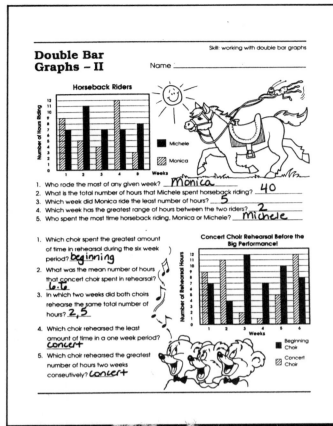

■ Michele
▨ Monica

1. Who rode the most of any given week? **Monica**
2. What is the total number of hours that Michele spent horseback riding? **40**
3. Which week did Monica ride the least number of hours? **5**
4. Which week has the greatest range of hours between the two riders? **2**
5. Who spent the most time horseback riding, Monica or Michele? **Michele**

Concert Choir Rehearsal Before the Big Performance!

1. Which choir spent the greatest amount of time in rehearsal during the six week period? **beginning**
2. What was the mean number of hours that concert choir spent in rehearsal? **6.6**
3. In which two weeks did both choirs rehearse the same total number of hours? **2, 5**
4. Which choir rehearsed the least amount of time in a one week period? **concert**
5. Which choir rehearsed the greatest number of hours two weeks consecutively? **Concert**

■ Beginning Choir
▨ Concert Choir

Page 13

Page 14

Pictographs

Skill: working with pictographs

Name _____

Favorite Subjects in Science
(The Fifth and Sixth Grades at Whataday Elementary)

Astronomy	
Geology	
Oceans	
Living Things	
Fossils	
Machines	

■ Represents 10 students' votes   ▨ Represents 5 students' votes

1. Which subject of science is the most popular at Whataday Elementary School? **astronomy**
2. Which one received the least number of votes? **machines**
3. How many students in all shared their opinion? **260**
4. How many students in all voted for oceans and geology? **80**
5. How many students said that the study of fossils was their favorite? **50**
6. What is your favorite area in science?
7. If you asked the students in your class, what would the majority say is their favorite area in science?

Favorite Free Time Recreation
(The Fifth and Sixth Grades at Whataday Elementary)

■ Represents 10 students' votes
▨ Represents 5 students' votes

Reading exciting books	
Rollerblading	
Skateboarding	
Playing piano	
Swimming	

1. How many students voted for reading exciting books? **60**
2. How many students voted for playing the piano? **75**
3. Which activity received the greatest number of votes? **piano**
4. How many more votes did swimming receive than skateboarding? **20**
5. How many students in all shared their opinion? **260**
6. What is the range of votes on this pictograph? **45**

Page 14

Page 15

Line Graphs

Skill: working with line graphs

Name _____

Falling Star (Meteor) Gazing Nights

1. How many more meteors were spotted on the second night than on the first? **12**
2. How many nights were a total of 16 falling stars observed? **2**
3. Which night were no meteors observed? **4**
4. On which two nights were two meteors observed? **3+8**
5. How many falling stars were observed altogether? **102**

Monica Goes Unicycle Riding!

1. How many seconds was Monica able to stay balanced on her first try? **10**
2. On her fourth try, was she able to stay on longer than her third try? **no**
3. In all her times riding, which time did she stay on for the longest time? **5**
4. What was the mean time that Monica remained on her unicycle? **35**
5. Which time did Monica remain on her unicycle longer, the fifth or seventh try? **5**

Page 15

Page 16

Double Line Graphs – I

Skill: working with double line graphs

Name _____

Continual Time Without Rest at Swim Team Workouts

—— Cyndi swimming in week number 2
—— Cyndi swimming in week number 1

1. On the very first day of workouts, how soon after Cyndi started did she need to take a rest? **5 min**
2. In week number one, how soon did Cyndi need to rest on day number three? **15 min**
3. How long could she go without rest on the third day of the second week? **35 min**
4. What is the range of week number one? **35**
5. What is the range of week two? **40**
6. Did Cyndi improve in both weeks? **yes**

Overseas Pen Pal Letters Received from France

—— Mr. Shoe's class
- - - Mrs. Write's class

1. Which class received 18 letters more often within a one month period? **Mr. Shoe**
2. Which class received the most letters the first month? **Mrs. Write** The last month? **Mrs. Write**
3. How many letters did Mrs. Write's class receive in all? **140**
4. Which class received more letters? **Mrs. Write**
5. Which class only received two letters in January, May and December? **Mr. Shoe**

Page 16

Page 17

Double Line Graphs – II

Skill: working with double line graphs

Name _____

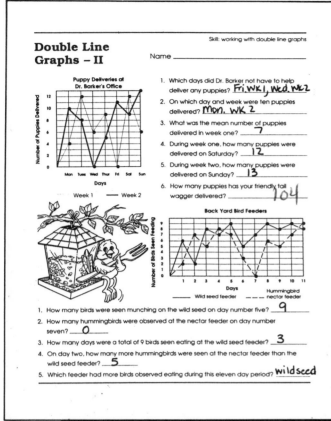

Puppy Deliveries at Dr. Barker's Office

Week 1 —— Week 2

Back Yard Bird Feeders

Wild seed feeder —— Hummingbird nectar feeder ---

1. Which days did Dr. Barker not have to help deliver any puppies? **Fri. WK 1, Wed. WK 2**
2. On which day and week were ten puppies delivered? **Mon. WK 2**
3. What was the mean number of puppies delivered in week one? **7**
4. During week one, how many puppies were delivered on Saturday? **12**
5. During week two, how many puppies were delivered on Sunday? **13**
6. How many puppies has your friendly tail wagger delivered? **104**

1. How many birds were seen munching on the wild seed on day number five? **9**
2. How many hummingbirds were observed at the nectar feeder on day number seven? **0**
3. How many days were a total of 9 birds seen eating at the wild seed feeder? **3**
4. On day two, how many more hummingbirds were seen at the nectar feeder than the wild seed feeder? **5**
5. Which feeder had more birds observed eating during this eleven day period? **wild seed**

Page 18

Circle Graphs – I

Skill: working with circle graphs

Name _____

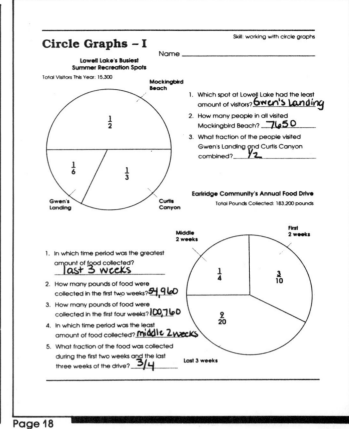

Lowell Lake's Busiest Summer Recreation Spots

Total Visitors This Year: 15,300

Mockingbird Beach — $\frac{1}{2}$
Gwen's Landing — $\frac{1}{6}$
Curtis Canyon — $\frac{1}{3}$

1. Which spot at Lowell Lake had the least amount of visitors? **Gwen's Landing**
2. How many people in all visited Mockingbird Beach? **7650**
3. What fraction of the people visited Gwen's Landing and Curtis Canyon combined? **½**

Earlridge Community's Annual Food Drive

Total Pounds Collected: 183,200 pounds

First 2 weeks — $\frac{3}{10}$
Middle 2 weeks — $\frac{1}{4}$
$\frac{2}{20}$
Last 3 weeks

1. In which time period was the greatest amount of food collected? **last 3 weeks**
2. How many pounds of food were collected in the first two weeks? **54,960**
3. How many pounds of food were collected in the first four weeks? **100,760**
4. In which time period was the least amount of food collected? **middle 2 weeks**
5. What fraction of the food was collected during the first two weeks and the last three weeks of the drive? **3/4**

Page 19

Circle Graphs – II

Skill: working with circle graphs

Name _____

Students Vote for Lunch Entrees at Sailboat Elementary School

Total Votes Counted: 600

5% — 30% — 20% — 35% — 10%

- Meat Loaf
- Macaroni and Cheese
- Chicken Nuggets
- Hamburgers
- Barbecue Chicken

1. Which entree received the most votes? **hamburgers**
2. How many votes were counted for meat loaf? **30**
3. Which entree received the second most popular amount of votes? **macaroni + cheese**
4. How many students voted for barbecue chicken? **120**
5. Which entree would have received the most votes if hamburgers and macaroni and cheese had not been listed in the poll? **barbecue chicken**
6. Which entree would you have voted for? _____ Which one is the most popular at your school? _____
7. How many students at Sailboat Elementary School voted for chicken nuggets? **60**

Field Trips This Year in Rollerblade Canyon School District

Total Trips: 900

5% — 25% — 20% — 10% — 40%

- Out-of-state Adventures
- Overnight Camping
- Symphony
- Wildlife Parks and Zoos
- Museums

1. What percent of the students had the privilege of exploring in out-of-state adventures? **5%**
2. How many field trips were taken to the symphony? **90**
3. Were more trips taken to the wildlife park and zoo, or to the museums and overnight camping combined? **museums + overnight camping**
4. How many overnight camping trips were taken? **180**

Page 20

Circle Graphs—III

Skill: working with circle graphs

Name _____

Mr. Manysmiles' Assignment Distribution

10% — 5% — 15% — 15% — 20% — 35%

- Science
- Drawing
- Reading
- Math
- Foreign Language
- Grammar

1. How many reading and grammar assignments were given altogether? **252**
2. What percent of the assignments were for science? **10**
3. How many math assignments were given? **252**
4. How many more foreign language assignments were given than drawing? **72**
5. How many drawing assignments were given altogether? **36**
6. What percent would have to be added to the number of science assignments given to equal those given in math? **25%**
7. If we add the reading and math assignments together, does this percentage equal more than the other subjects combined? **yes**

Heather Cove Music Shop's Instrument Rental's Since 1980

20% — 45% — 30% — 5%

- Strings
- Woodwinds
- Percussion
- Brass

1. How many string instruments have been rented since 1980? **4752**
2. Which type of instrument has been rented the most? **brass**
3. Which instrument has been rented the least number of times? **percussion**
4. How many string and woodwind instruments have been rented altogether since 1980? **11,880**
5. If twice as many woodwinds had been rented than brass instruments, would this exceed the number of brass instruments rented? If so, by how many? **3564**
6. Which instrument do you play in your band or orchestra? _____
7. Which sounds the most beautiful to you? _____

Answer Key

Page 21

Metric Units of Length - I

Name _____

1 cm = 10 mm

Hint: If it's .5 or greater, round up to the next cm.
If it's less than .5, round down.

A. Complete each conversion.

30 mm = **3** cm 8.5 cm = **85** mm 50 mm = **5** cm
80 mm = **8** cm 38 mm = **3.8** cm 5.9 cm = **59** mm
14.2 cm = **142** mm 4.7 cm = **47** mm 900 mm = **90** cm
65 mm = **6.5** cm 3.2 cm = **32** mm 2.9 cm = **29** mm

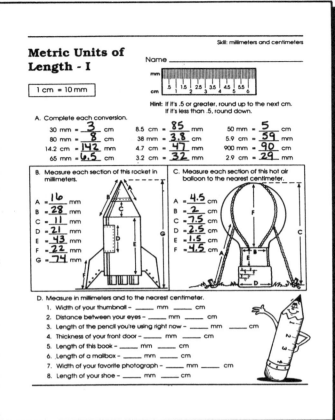

B. Measure each section of this rocket in millimeters.

A = **16** mm
B = **28** mm
C = **11** mm
D = **21** mm
E = **43** mm
F = **22** mm
G = **74** mm

C. Measure each section of this hot air balloon to the nearest centimeter.

A = **4.5** cm
B = **2** cm
C = **7.5** cm
D = **2.5** cm
E = **1.5** cm
F = **4.5** cm

D. Measure in millimeters and to the nearest centimeter.

1. Width of your thumbnail – _____ mm _____ cm
2. Distance between your eyes – _____ mm _____ cm
3. Length of the pencil you're using right now – _____ mm _____ cm
4. Thickness of your front door – _____ mm _____ cm
5. Length of this book – _____ mm _____ cm
6. Length of a mailbox – _____ mm _____ cm
7. Width of your favorite photograph – _____ mm _____ cm
8. Length of your shoe – _____ mm _____ cm

Page 22

Metric Units of Length - II

Name _____

1 cm	=	10 mm
1 m	=	100 cm
1 km	=	1,000 m

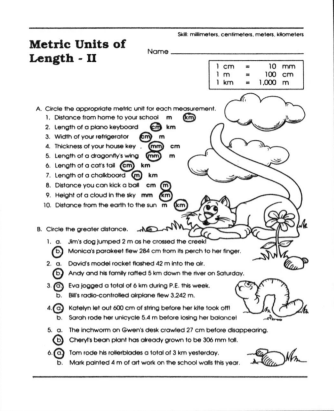

A. Circle the appropriate metric unit for each measurement.

1. Distance from home to your school m **(km)**
2. Length of a piano keyboard **(cm)** km
3. Width of your refrigerator **(cm)** m
4. Thickness of your house key **(mm)** cm
5. Length of a dragonfly's wing **(mm)** m
6. Length of a cat's tail **(cm)** km
7. Length of a chalkboard **(m)** km
8. Distance you can kick a ball cm **(m)**
9. Height of a cloud in the sky mm **(m)**
10. Distance from the earth to the sun m **(km)**

B. Circle the greater distance.

1. a. Jim's dog jumped 2 m as he crossed the creek!
   (b.) Monica's parakeet flew 284 cm from its perch to her finger.
2. a. David's model rocket flashed 42 m into the air.
   (b.) Andy and his family rafted 5 km down the river on Saturday.
3. **(a.)** Eva jogged a total of 6 km during P.E. this week.
   b. Bill's radio-controlled airplane flew 3,242 m.
4. **(a.)** Katelyn let out 600 cm of string before her kite took off!
   b. Sarah rode her unicycle 5.4 m before losing her balance!
5. a. The inchworm on Gwen's desk crawled 27 cm before disappearing.
   (b.) Cheryl's bean plant has already grown to be 306 mm tall.
6. **(a.)** Tom rode his rollerblades a total of 3 km yesterday.
   b. Mark painted 4 m of art work on the school walls this year.

Page 23

Metric Units of Capacity

Name _____

1 mL = 0.001 L

A. Match each diagram with the correct capacity.

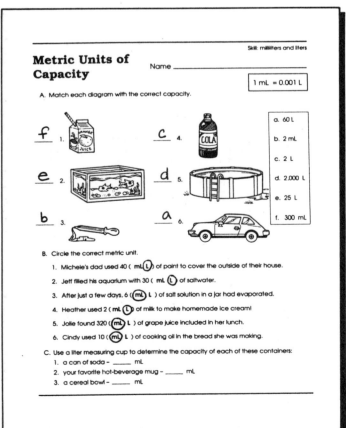

f 1.
c 4.
e 2.
d 5.
b 3.
a 6.

a. 60 L
b. 2 mL
c. 2 L
d. 2,000 L
e. 25 L
f. 300 mL

B. Circle the correct metric unit.

1. Michele's dad used 40 (mL **(L)**) of paint to cover the outside of their house.
2. Jeff filled his aquarium with 30 (mL **(L)**) of saltwater.
3. After just a few days, 6 (**(mL)** L) of salt solution in a jar had evaporated.
4. Heather used 2 (mL **(L)**) of milk to make homemade ice cream!
5. Jolie found 320 (**(mL)** L) of grape juice included in her lunch.
6. Cindy used 10 (**(mL)** L) of cooking oil in the bread she was making.

C. Use a liter measuring cup to determine the capacity of each of these containers:

1. a can of soda – _____ mL
2. your favorite hot-beverage mug – _____ mL
3. a cereal bowl – _____ mL

Page 24

Metric Units of Mass

Name _____

1,000 mg	=	1 g
1,000 g	=	1 kg

A. Astronauts aboard the spacecraft "Moon Crater" accidentally left the gravity machine off when they bunked down for the night. What mass would each of these floating items have on earth? milligram (mg), gram (g), or kilogram (kg)

3 **kg** 50 **mg**
30 **mg** 60 **kg**
50 **g** 30 **g** 1 **kg** 2 **kg**

B. Solve the following problems.

1. Kelly's dog "Barksinger" weighs a total of 40 kg while soaking wet during a bath. After drying off, he loses 3,000 g. How much does Barksinger now weigh? **37 kg**
2. Carolyn picks 10 kg of oranges from her tree. After squeezing out the juice, she discovers that the leftover rinds weigh 2,000 g. How many kilograms of juice are there? **8 kg**
3. On Wednesday, Al ran a magnet through the sand to extract iron filings. He collected a total of 720 g of iron. On Thursday, he extracted another 1,280 g. How many kilograms did he extract altogether? **2 kg**
4. Marnie picked 82,000 g of watermelon for the family picnic. How many kilograms does this equal? **82 kg**

C. Circle the appropriate unit of mass.

1. Katy poured 350 (**(mg)** g kg) of salt on her steak.
2. Casandra lugged home 4 (mg g **(kg)**) of books in her backpack today.
3. Jonathan was pleased to find 10 (mg **(g)** kg) of black olives on his pizza?
4. Brittainy was happy to find that her new skates only weighed 2 (mg g **(kg)**).

Answer Key

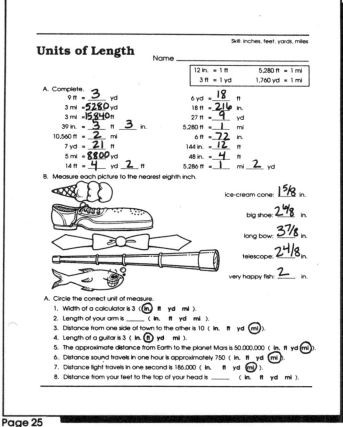

Units of Length

Skill: inches, feet, yards, miles

Name _____

12 in. = 1 ft	5,280 ft = 1 mi
3 ft = 1 yd	1,760 yd = 1 mi

A. Complete.

9 ft = **3** yd
3 mi = **5280** yd
3 mi = **15840** ft
39 in. = **3** ft **3** in.
10,560 ft = **2** mi
7 yd = **21** ft
5 mi = **8800** yd
14 ft = **4** yd **2** ft

6 yd = **18** ft
18 ft = **216** in.
27 ft = **9** yd
5,280 ft = **1** mi
6 ft = **72** in.
144 in. = **12** ft
48 in. = **4** ft
5,286 ft = **1** mi **2** yd

B. Measure each picture to the nearest eighth inch.

ice-cream cone: **1 5/8** in.
big shoe: **2 4/8** in.
long bow: **3 7/8** in.
telescope: **24/8** in.
very happy fish: **2** in.

A. Circle the correct unit of measure.
1. Width of a calculator is 3 (**in.** ft yd mi).
2. Length of your arm is _____ (**in.** ft yd mi).
3. Distance from one side of town to the other is 10 (in. ft yd **mi**).
4. Length of a guitar is 3 (in. **ft** yd mi).
5. The approximate distance from Earth to the planet Mars is 50,000,000 (in. ft yd **mi**).
6. Distance sound travels in one hour is approximately 750 (in. ft yd **mi**).
7. Distance light travels in one second is 186,000 (in. ft yd **mi**).
8. Distance from your feet to the top of your head is _____ (in. **ft** yd mi).

Page 25

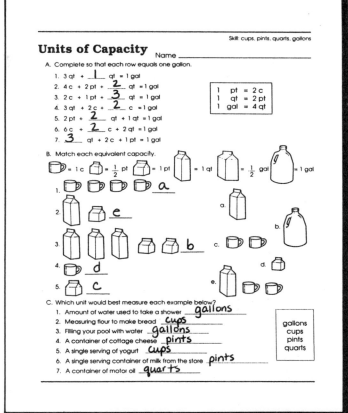

Units of Capacity

Skill: cups, pints, quarts, gallons

Name _____

A. Complete so that each row equals one gallon.
1. 3 qt + **1** qt = 1 gal
2. 4 c + 2 pt + **2** qt = 1 gal
3. 2 c + 1 pt + **3** qt = 1 gal
4. 3 qt + 2 c + **2** c = 1 gal
5. 2 pt + **2** qt + 1 qt = 1 gal
6. 6 c + **2** c + 2 qt = 1 gal
7. **3** qt + 2 c + 1 pt = 1 gal

| 1 pt = 2 c |
| 1 qt = 2 pt |
| 1 gal = 4 qt |

B. Match each equivalent capacity.
= 1 c   = ½ pt   = 1 pt   = 1 qt   = ½ gal   = 1 gal
1. **a**
2. **e**
3. **b**
4. **d**
5. **c**

C. Which unit would best measure each example below?
1. Amount of water used to take a shower **gallons**
2. Measuring flour to make bread **cups**
3. Filling your pool with water **gallons**
4. A container of cottage cheese **pints**
5. A single serving of yogurt **cups**
6. A single serving container of milk from the store **pints**
7. A container of motor oil **quarts**

| gallons |
| cups |
| pints |
| quarts |

Page 26

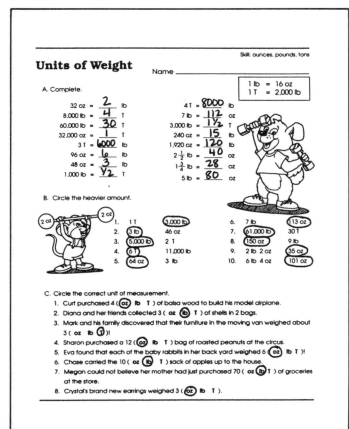

Units of Weight

Skill: ounces, pounds, tons

Name _____

| 1 lb = 16 oz |
| 1 T = 2,000 lb |

A. Complete.

32 oz = **2** lb
8,000 lb = **4** T
60,000 lb = **30** T
32,000 oz = **1** T
3 T = **6000** lb
96 oz = **6** lb
48 oz = **3** lb
1,000 lb = **½** T

4 T = **8000** lb
7 lb = **112** oz
3,000 lb = **1½** T
240 oz = **15** lb
1,920 oz = **120** lb
2 ½ lb = **40** oz
1 ¾ lb = **28** oz
5 lb = **80** oz

B. Circle the heavier amount.
1. 1 T / **3,000 lb**
2. **3 lb** / 46 oz
3. **5,000 lb** / 2 T
4. **6 lb** / 11,000 lb
5. **64 oz** / 3 lb
6. 7 lb / **113 oz**
7. **61,000 lb** / 30 T
8. **150 oz** / 9 lb
9. 2 lb 2 oz / **35 oz**
10. 6 lb 4 oz / **101 oz**

C. Circle the correct unit of measurement.
1. Curt purchased 4 (**oz** lb T) of balsa wood to build his model airplane.
2. Diana and her friends collected 3 (oz **lb** T) of shells in 2 bags.
3. Mark and his family discovered that their furniture in the moving van weighed about 3 (oz lb **T**)!
4. Sharon purchased a 12 (**oz** lb T) bag of roasted peanuts at the circus.
5. Eva found that each of the baby rabbits in her back yard weighed 6 (**oz** lb T)!
6. Chase carried the 10 (oz **lb** T) sack of apples up to the house.
7. Megan could not believe her mother had just purchased 70 (oz **lb** T) of groceries at the store.
8. Crystal's brand new earrings weighed 3 (**oz** lb T).

Page 27

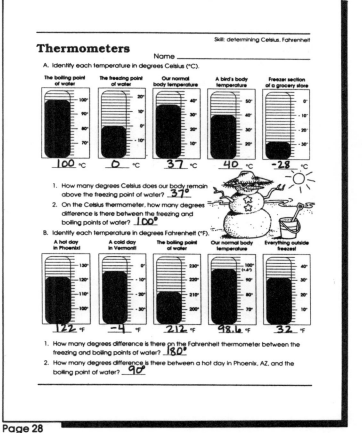

Thermometers

Skill: determining Celsius, Fahrenheit

Name _____

A. Identify each temperature in degrees Celsius (°C).

The boiling point of water: **100** °C
The freezing point of water: **0** °C
Our normal body temperature: **37** °C
A bird's body temperature: **40** °C
Freezer section of a grocery store: **-28** °C

1. How many degrees Celsius does our body remain above the freezing point of water? **37°**
2. On the Celsius thermometer, how many degrees difference is there between the freezing and boiling points of water? **100°**

B. Identify each temperature in degrees Fahrenheit (°F).

A hot day in Phoenix!: **122** °F
A cold day in Vermont!: **-4** °F
The boiling point of water: **212** °F
Our normal body temperature: **98.6** °F
Everything outside freezes!: **32** °F

1. How many degrees difference is there on the Fahrenheit thermometer between the freezing and boiling points of water? **180°**
2. How many degrees difference is there between a hot day in Phoenix, AZ, and the boiling point of water? **90°**

Page 28

Answer Key

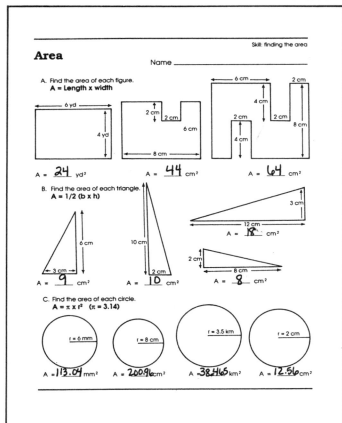

Area
Skill: finding the area

Name _____

A. Find the area of each figure.
A = Length x width

A = **24** yd²   A = **44** cm²   A = **64** cm²

B. Find the area of each triangle.
A = 1/2 (b x h)

A = **9** cm²   A = **10** cm²   A = **8** cm²   A = **18** cm²

C. Find the area of each circle.
A = π x r²   (π = 3.14)

A = **113.04** mm²   A = **200.96** cm²   A = **38.465** km²   A = **12.56** cm²

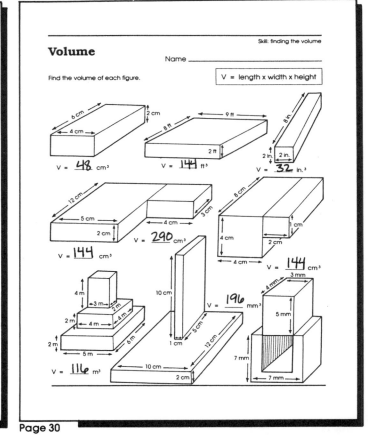

Volume
Skill: finding the volume

Name _____

Find the volume of each figure.

$$V = \text{length x width x height}$$

V = **48** cm³   V = **144** ft³   V = **32** in.³

V = **144** cm³   V = **290** cm³   V = **144** cm³

V = **116** m³   V = **196** mm³

Points, Lines, Rays, Line Segments and Planes
Skill: identifying geometric figures

Name _____

Match.

Point S = •S	Ray XY = $\overrightarrow{XY}$
Line CD = $\overleftrightarrow{CD}$	Line segment BC = $\overline{BC}$

1. **G**
2. **B**
3. **L**
4. **H**
5. **N**
6. **Q**
7. **O**
8. **I**
9. **C**

10. **m**
11. **A**
12. **J**
13. **E**
14. **F**
15. **P**
16. **D**
17. **K**

A. $\overrightarrow{GH}$
B. Point Q
C. Plane E
D. Plane D
E. Point A
F. $\overrightarrow{OP}$
G. $\overleftrightarrow{LM}$
H. $\overrightarrow{YZ}$
I. $\overleftrightarrow{MN}$
J. $\overleftrightarrow{HI}$
K. $\overleftrightarrow{JK}$
L. $\overrightarrow{RS}$
M. $\overleftrightarrow{PQ}$
N. $\overrightarrow{TU}$
O. Point X
P. $\overline{QR}$
Q. Plane B

Parallel, Intersecting and Perpendicular Lines and Line Segments
Skill: identifying geometric figures

Name _____

$\overleftrightarrow{AB}$ is perpendicular to $\overleftrightarrow{CD}$ = $\overleftrightarrow{AB} \perp \overleftrightarrow{CD}$	$\overline{AB}$ is parallel to $\overline{CD}$ = $\overline{AB}$ ‖ $\overline{CD}$

Circle the correct name for each figure.

1. (QR Intersects ST) $\overleftrightarrow{QR}$ ‖ $\overleftrightarrow{ST}$
2. $\overline{BC}$ ‖ $\overline{DE}$ (BC ‖ DE)
3. $\overline{HI} \perp \overline{JK}$ (HI intersects JK)
4. (CD ⊥ EF)   CD ‖ EF
5. EF intersects GH   (EF ‖ GH)

6. (WX ⊥ YZ) $\overleftrightarrow{WX}$ $\overleftrightarrow{YZ}$
7. $\overline{AB}$ intersects $\overline{CD}$ (AB ‖ CD)
8. $\overline{TU} \perp \overline{VW}$ (TU ⊥ VW) $\overleftrightarrow{TU}$ ‖ $\overleftrightarrow{VW}$
9. $\overline{DE} \perp \overline{FG}$ (DE intersects FG at H)

IF8747 Math Topics

Answer Key

Working With Geometric Figures

Name _____

Use this figure to answer the questions below.

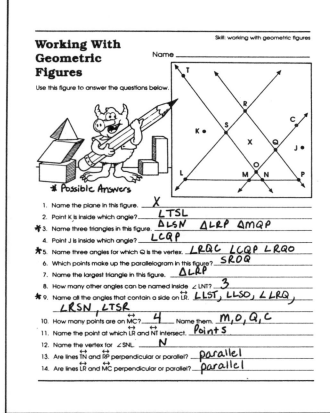

✱ Possible Answers

1. Name the plane in this figure. __X__
2. Point K is inside which angle? __LTSL__
✱ 3. Name three triangles in this figure. __ΔLSN   ΔLRP   ΔMQP__
4. Point J is inside which angle? __LCQP__
✱ 5. Name three angles for which Q is the vertex. __LRQC   LCQP   LRQO__
6. Which points make up the parallelogram in this figure? __SROQ__
7. Name the largest triangle in this figure. __ΔLRP__
8. How many other angles can be named inside ∠LNT? __3__
✱ 9. Name all the angles that contain a side on L̄R̄. __LLST, LLSO, ∠LRQ,__
   __LRSN , LTSR__
10. How many points are on M̄C̄? __4__   Name them. __m, o, Q, C__
11. Name the point at which L̄R̄ and N̄T̄ intersect. __Points__
12. Name the vertex for ∠SNL. __N__
13. Are lines T̄N̄ and R̄P̄ perpendicular or parallel? __parallel__
14. Are lines L̄R̄ and M̄C̄ perpendicular or parallel? __parallel__

Acute, Right and Obtuse Angles

Name _____

Acute Angle: Less than 90°	Obtuse Angle: Greater than 90°, less than 180°
Right Angle: 90°	

Label each angle.

1. obtuse
2. acute
3. acute
4. right
5. obtuse
6. acute
7. obtuse
8. right
9. obtuse
10. acute
11. right
12. acute

Angle Measurement

Name _____

The **degree** is the unit used to measure angles.

Measure the following angles using a protractor.

1. 62°
2. 103°
3. 27°
4. 70°
5. 90°
6. 130°
7. 162°
8. 47°

Draw the angles given using a protractor.

1. 70°
2. 120°
3. 40°
4. 90°
5. 150°
6. 110°

Congruent Figures – I

Name _____

Are these congruent? Write **yes** or **no**.

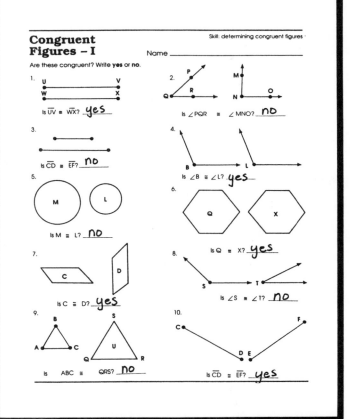

1. Is ŪV̄ ≅ W̄X̄? __yes__
2. Is ∠PQR ≅ ∠MNO? __no__
3. Is C̄D̄ ≅ ĒF̄? __no__
4. Is ∠B ≅ ∠L? __yes__
5. Is M ≅ L? __no__
6. Is Q ≅ X? __yes__
7. Is C ≅ D? __yes__
8. Is ∠S ≅ ∠T? __no__
9. Is ABC ≅ QRS? __no__
10. Is C̄D̄ ≅ ĒF̄? __yes__

111   IF8747 Math Topics

Answer Key

©1992 Instructional Fair, Inc.

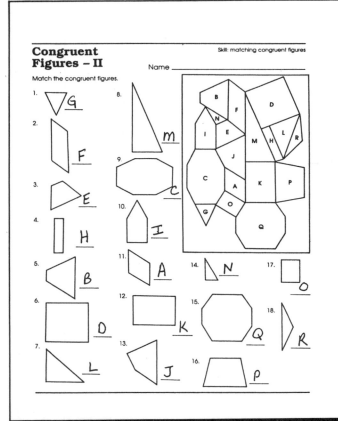

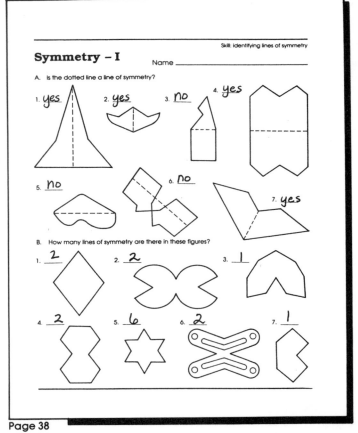

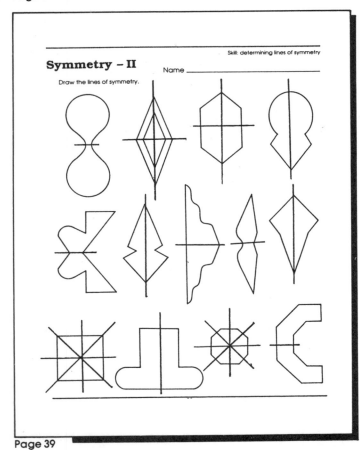

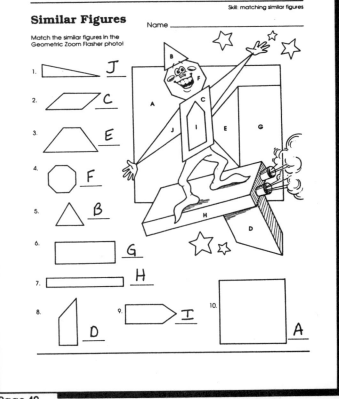

Page 37

Page 38

Page 39

Page 40

112

IF8747 Math Topics

Answer Key

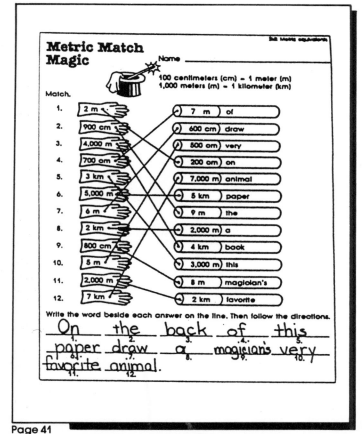

Metric Match Magic

Name _____

100 centimeters (cm) = 1 meter (m)
1,000 meters (m) = 1 kilometer (km)

Match.

1. 2 m
2. 900 cm
3. 4,000 m
4. 700 cm
5. 3 km
6. 5,000 m
7. 6 m
8. 2 km
9. 800 cm
10. 5 m
11. 2,000 m
12. 7 km

- 7 m — of
- 600 cm — draw
- 500 cm — very
- 200 cm — on
- 7,000 m — animal
- 5 km — paper
- 9 m — the
- 2,000 m — a
- 4 km — book
- 3,000 m — this
- 8 m — magician's
- 2 km — favorite

Write the word beside each answer on the line. Then follow the directions.

On the back of this paper draw a magician's very favorite animal.

Page 41

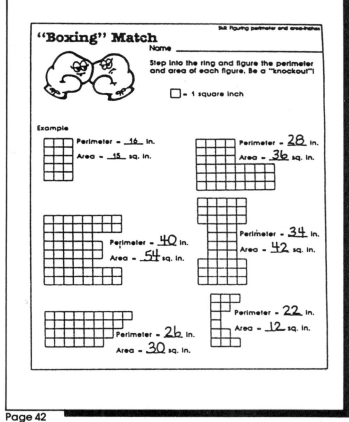

"Boxing" Match

Name _____

Step into the ring and figure the perimeter and area of each figure. Be a "knockout"!

□ = 1 square inch

Example

- Perimeter = 16 in.   Area = 15 sq. in.
- Perimeter = 28 in.   Area = 36 sq. in.
- Perimeter = 40 in.   Area = 54 sq. in.
- Perimeter = 34 in.   Area = 42 sq. in.
- Perimeter = 26 in.   Area = 30 sq. in.
- Perimeter = 22 in.   Area = 12 sq. in.

Page 42

Yard Work

Name _____

1 ft. = 12 in.
1 yd. = 36 in.
1 yd. = 3 ft.

Try this "yard" work by filling the blanks with "blooming" good answers.

3 ft. = 36 in.	4 yd. = 144 in.	5 yd. = 15 ft.
6 ft. = 72 in.	7 yd. = 252 in.	9 yd. = 27 ft.
2 ft. = 24 in.	3 yd. = 108 in.	3 yd. = 9 ft.
4 ft. = 48 in.	5 yd. = 180 in.	7 yd. = 21 ft.
7 ft. = 84 in.	6 yd. = 216 in.	8 yd. = 24 ft.
5 ft. = 60 in.	8 yd. = 288 in.	4 yd. = 12 ft.

"Dig" deeper on these! Complete.

21 in. = 1 ft. and 9 in.	1 ft. and 4 in. = 16 in.
16 in. = 1 ft. and 4 in.	2 ft. and 6 in. = 30 in.
26 in. = 2 ft. and 2 in.	1 ft. and 10 in. = 22 in.
14 in. = 1 ft. and 2 in.	2 ft. and 8 in. = 32 in.

Page 43

Add or Subtract?

Learn these key words. They will help you know when to add and when to subtract.
Addition key words: in all, altogether   Subtraction key words: more, left
Circle the key words and solve the story problems.

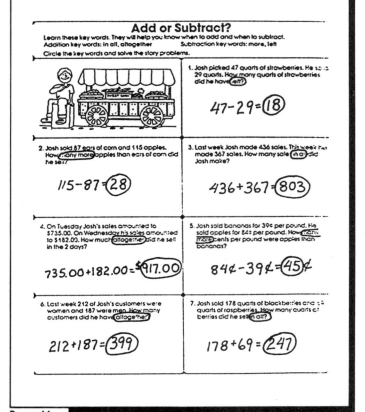

1. Josh picked 47 quarts of strawberries. He sold 29 quarts. How many quarts of strawberries did he have left?

$47 - 29 = 18$

2. Josh sold 87 ears of corn and 115 apples. How many more apples than ears of corn did he sell?

$115 - 87 = 28$

3. Last week Josh made 436 sales. This week he made 367 sales. How many sales in all did Josh make?

$436 + 367 = 803$

4. On Tuesday Josh's sales amounted to $735.00. On Wednesday his sales amounted to $182.00. How much altogether did he sell in the 2 days?

$735.00 + 182.00 = \$917.00$

5. Josh sold bananas for 39¢ per pound. He sold apples for 84¢ per pound. How many more cents per pound were apples than bananas?

$84¢ - 39¢ = 45¢$

6. Last week 212 of Josh's customers were women and 187 were men. How many customers did he have altogether?

$212 + 187 = 399$

7. Josh sold 178 quarts of blackberries and 69 quarts of raspberries. How many quarts of berries did he sell in all?

$178 + 69 = 247$

Page 44

©1992 Instructional Fair, Inc.   113   IF8747 Math Topics

Answer Key

Page 45

Multiply or Divide?

Learn these key words. They will help you know when to multiply and when to divide.
Multiplication key words: in all, altogether, times and each
Division key words: per, each

Circle the key words and solve the story problems.

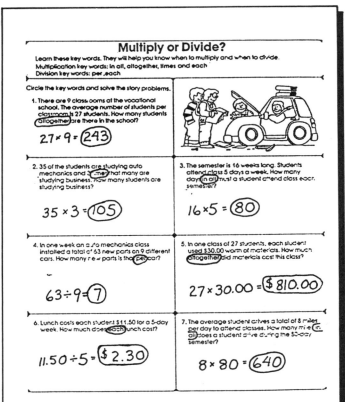

1. There are 9 classrooms at the vocational school. The average number of students per classroom is 27 students. How many students altogether are there in the school?

$27 \times 9 = \boxed{243}$

2. 35 of the students are studying auto mechanics and 3 times that many are studying business. How many students are studying business?

$35 \times 3 = \boxed{105}$

3. The semester is 16 weeks long. Students attend class 5 days a week. How many days in all must a student attend class each semester?

$16 \times 5 = \boxed{80}$

4. In one week an auto mechanics class installed a total of 63 new parts on 9 different cars. How many new parts is that per car?

$63 \div 9 = \boxed{7}$

5. In one class of 27 students, each student used $30.00 worth of materials. How much altogether did materials cost this class?

$27 \times 30.00 = \boxed{\$810.00}$

6. Lunch costs each student $11.50 for a 5-day week. How much does each lunch cost?

$11.50 \div 5 = \boxed{\$2.30}$

7. The average student drives a total of 8 miles per day to attend classes. How many miles in all does a student drive during the 80-day semester?

$8 \times 80 = \boxed{640}$

Page 46

Time — I

Fill in the clocks and solve the problems. The first one has been done for you.

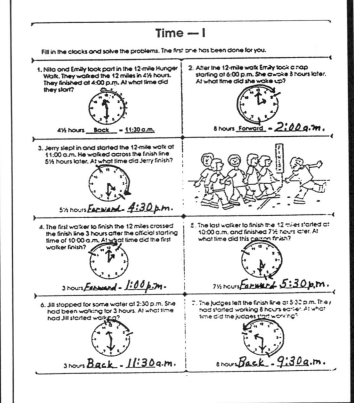

1. Nita and Emily took part in the 12-mile Hunger Walk. They walked the 12 miles in 4½ hours. They finished at 4:00 p.m. At what time did they start?

4½ hours __Back__ = 11:30 a.m.

2. After the 12-mile walk Emily took a nap starting at 6:00 p.m. She awoke 8 hours later. At what time did she wake up?

8 hours __Forward__ = 2:00 a.m.

3. Jerry slept in and started the 12-mile walk at 11:00 a.m. He walked across the finish line 5½ hours later. At what time did Jerry finish?

5½ hours __Forward__ = 4:30 p.m.

4. The first walker to finish the 12 miles crossed the finish line 3 hours after the official starting time of 10:00 a.m. At what time did the first walker finish?

3 hours __Forward__ = 1:00 p.m.

5. The last walker to finish the 12 miles started at 10:00 a.m. and finished 7½ hours later. At what time did this person finish?

7½ hours __Forward__ = 5:30 p.m.

6. Jill stopped for some water at 2:30 p.m. She had been walking for 3 hours. At what time had Jill started walking?

3 hours __Back__ = 11:30 a.m.

7. The judges left the finish line at 5:30 p.m. They had started working 8 hours earlier. At what time did the judges start working?

8 hours __Back__ = 9:30 a.m.

Page 47

Time — II

Solve the following problems.

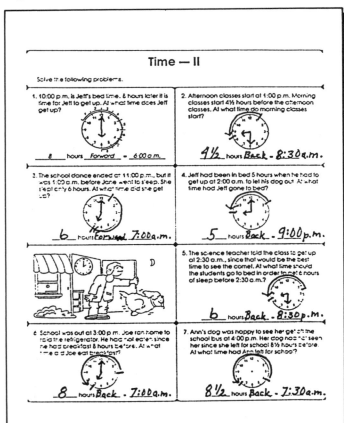

1. 10:00 p.m. is Jeff's bed time. 8 hours later it is time for Jeff to get up. At what time does Jeff get up?

8 hours __Forward__ = 6:00 a.m.

2. Afternoon classes start at 1:00 p.m. Morning classes start 4½ hours before the afternoon classes. At what time do morning classes start?

4½ hours __Back__ = 8:30 a.m.

3. The school dance ended at 11:00 p.m., but it was 1:00 a.m. before Jane went to sleep. She slept only 6 hours. At what time did she get up?

6 hours __Forward__ = 7:00 a.m.

4. Jeff had been in bed 5 hours when he had to get up at 2:00 a.m. to let his dog out. At what time had Jeff gone to bed?

5 hours __Back__ = 9:00 p.m.

5. The science teacher told the class to get up at 2:30 a.m., since that would be the best time to see the comet. At what time should the students go to bed in order to get 6 hours of sleep before 2:30 a.m.?

6 hours __Back__ = 8:30 p.m.

6. School was out at 3:00 p.m. Joe ran home to raid the refrigerator. He had not eaten since he had breakfast 8 hours before. At what time did Joe eat breakfast?

8 hours __Back__ = 7:00 a.m.

7. Ann's dog was happy to see her get off the school bus at 4:00 p.m. Her dog had not seen her since she left for school 8½ hours before. At what time had Ann left for school?

8½ hours __Back__ = 7:30 a.m.

Page 48

Time — III

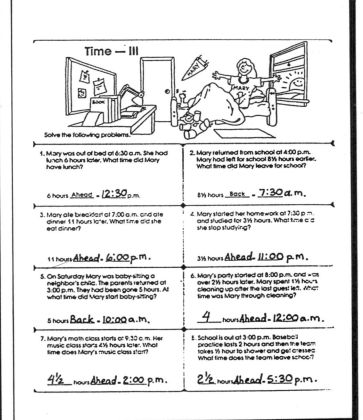

Solve the following problems.

1. Mary was out of bed at 6:30 a.m. She had lunch 6 hours later. What time did Mary have lunch?

6 hours __Ahead__ = 12:30 p.m.

2. Mary returned from school at 4:00 p.m. Mary had left for school 8½ hours earlier. What time did Mary leave for school?

8½ hours __Back__ = 7:30 a.m.

3. Mary ate breakfast at 7:00 a.m. and ate dinner 11 hours later. What time did she eat dinner?

11 hours __Ahead__ = 6:00 p.m.

4. Mary started her homework at 7:30 p.m. and studied for 3½ hours. What time did she stop studying?

3½ hours __Ahead__ = 11:00 p.m.

5. On Saturday Mary was baby-sitting a neighbor's child. The parents returned at 3:00 p.m. They had been gone 5 hours. At what time did Mary start baby-sitting?

5 hours __Back__ = 10:00 a.m.

6. Mary's party started at 8:00 p.m. and was over 2½ hours later. Mary spent 1½ hours cleaning up after the last guest left. What time was Mary through cleaning?

4 hours __Ahead__ = 12:00 a.m.

7. Mary's math class starts at 9:30 a.m. Her music class starts 4½ hours later. What time does Mary's music class start?

4½ hours __Ahead__ = 2:00 p.m.

8. School is out at 3:00 p.m. Baseball practice lasts 2 hours and then the team takes ½ hour to shower and get dressed. What time does the team leave school?

2½ hours __Ahead__ = 5:30 p.m.

©1992 Instructional Fair, Inc.   IF8747 Math Topics

Answer Key

More Than One Step — I

Solve the following problems.

1. Harvey took 12 cub scouts to the zoo. Admission to the zoo is $2.50 per person. He also bought each cub scout a 50¢ soft drink. What was Harvey's cost, not including his own admission, for this day at the zoo?

step 1: 2.50   step 2: 12   answer **$36.00**
+0.50   x 3
3.00   36

2. The 12 cub scouts must each work on community projects at least 12 hours each month. What is the fewest number of hours altogether the cub scouts work on these projects in a year?

12   144
x 12   x 12
144   **(1,728)**

3. The scouts plan to have pancake breakfasts to raise money to buy new uniforms and to pay for a week at camp. Camp costs $35.00 per week for each scout. New uniforms cost $12.00 each. How much money must be raised for all 12 scouts to go to camp, and for 6 scouts to get new uniforms?

35.00   12.00   420.00
x 12   x 6   + 72.00
420.00   72.00   **$492.00**

4. A local car dealer loaned a van to the scout troop for the trip to camp. The van gets 14 miles per gallon of gasoline. Gasoline costs $1.10 per gallon. The trip to camp and back will cover 182 miles. How much will the trip cost in gasoline?

13   1.10
14)182   x 13
$14.30

5. Food at the camp costs $5.25 per scout per day. How much will it cost to feed all 12 scouts for one week?

5.25   63.00
x 12   x 7
63.00   **$441.00**

Page 49

More Than One Step — II

Solve the following problems.

1. The local police department has 52 members. ¼ of the police are women. ⅓ of the men are over 45 years of age. How many of the men are over 45?

Step 1: 4)52   Step 2: 3 x 13 = **39**
Step 3: 3)39   Step 4: 2 x 13 = **26**

2. In one week the police investigated 4 times as many auto wrecks and fires combined as burglaries. They were called to 94 wrecks and 82 fires. How many burglaries did they investigate?

94 + 82 = 176, 176 ÷ 4 = **44**

3. The police were called to investigate 42 fights where the people fighting were not related. They investigated 25 times that many family arguments. How many fights in all did the police investigate?

42 x 25 = 1,050
1,050 + 42 = **1,092**

4. The police issued 480 parking tickets and 124 speeding tickets. "Driving under the influence" charges totaled ¼ as many as the number of speeding tickets. How many tickets were issued in all?

124 ÷ 4 = 31
480 + 124 + 31 = **635**

5. Last week ¾ of the 124 speeders and ⅓ of the 72 jay walkers caught were second offenders and had to attend safety school. How many people altogether had to attend safety school?

124 ÷ 4 = 31   72 ÷ 3 = 24
31 x 3 = 93   93 + 24 = **117**

6. The health insurance plan costs the city $27.00 per month for each of the 52 police force members. Life insurance costs ⅓ as much. How much is spent each year on insurance for the police force?

(52 x 27.00) ÷ 3 = 468
1404 + 468 = **$1,872**

7. The city bought 7 new police cars that cost $16,500.00 each. 7 old police cars brought $3,400.00 each when traded in on new ones. How much was paid for the 7 new cars after the trade-in?

7 x 16,500 = 115,500
7 x 3,400 = 23,800 **$91,700.00**

8. The banquet for 2 retiring police officers was attended by 250 local residents. Each resident paid $12.50 for the dinner. $500.00 of the money collected was spent for gifts for the retirees. How much was left to pay for the banquet?

(250 x 12.50) − 500 = **$2,625.00**

Page 50

More Than One Step — III

Solve the following problems.

1. Of 6 dinner guests, 2 ordered steaks at $15.95 each, 1 ordered flounder at $12.50 and the other 3 ordered shrimp at $9.95 each. What was their total bill?

Step 1: 15.95   Step 2: 9.95
x 2   x 3
31.90   29.85
Step 3: 31.90 + 29.85 + 12.50 = **$74.25**

2. At the next table the waitress received orders for 2 soup-and-salad bars at $3.95 each, and 2 sandwich-and-salad bars at $4.95 each. What was the total bill for this table?

3.95   4.95
x 2   x 2
7.90 + 9.90 = **$17.80**

3. The waitress served 3 other tables whose total bills were $62.90, $38.45 and $24.85. If each table tips her 15% of the total bill, how much in tips will the waitress receive?

62.90 + 38.45 + 24.85 =
126.20   126.20 x .15 = **$18.93**

4. For group parties 15% of the bill is automatically added as a tip. One party had a food bill of $382.50. Another party's bill came to ½ of that amount. How much in tips altogether did the waitress receive from these parties?

382.50 ÷ 2 = 191.25
(382.50 + 191.25) x .15 = **$86.06**

5. The restaurant is open 7 days each week. On an average day 250 cups of coffee are served at 60¢ per cup. How much money is collected for coffee each week?

250 x .60 = 150
150 x 7 = **$1,050.00**

6. The average lunch crowd has 84 guests ordering the soup-and-salad bar at $3.95 each. How much is spent for the soup-and-salad bar in a 7-day week?

84 x 3.95 = 331.80
331.80 x 7 = **$2,322.60**

7. During an average breakfast, 45 orders of pancakes and sausage at $3.25 each are filled. This amounts to how much money over 30 days?

45 x 3.25 = 146.25
146.25 x 30 = **$4,387.50**

8. The restaurant has 12 waitresses each receiving $4.00 per hour in wages. The rest of their pay comes from tips from the guests. Each waitress works 40 hours per week. How much in all does the management pay the waitresses each week?

(12 x 40) x 4.00 = **$1,920.00**

Page 51

Multi-Step and Multi-Method

Solve the following problems.

1. Bill rides the bus to and from school each day. The bus fare is 20¢ each way. How much does Bill spend on bus fare during 20 days?

step 1: 20¢ + 20¢ = **40¢**
step 2: 20 x (step 1) **$8.00**

2. Find another way to solve problem #1.

step 1: 20 x 20¢ = **$4.00**
step 2: 2 x (step 1) **$8.00**

3. Bill spends $2.75 for lunch at a fast food diner. Lunch in the school cafeteria costs $1.30. How much could Bill save by eating in the school cafeteria instead for 5 days?

step 1: 2.75   step 2: 1.45
− 1.30   x 5
1.45   **$7.25**

4. Find another way to solve problem #3.

2.75   1.30   13.75
x 5   x 5   − 6.50
13.75   6.50   **$7.25**

5. The 5 girls each had a soft drink at 45¢ each and a bag of fries at 50¢ each. The 5 boys each had a soft drink at 55¢ each and ice cream at 70¢ each. How much more did the boys spend in all than the girls?

.45   .55   1.25   .30
+.50   +.70   − .95   x 5
.95   1.25   .30   **$1.50**

6. Find another way to solve problem #5.

.45   .55   .95   1.25
+.50   +.70   x 5   x 5
.95   1.25   4.75   6.25
6.25 − 4.75 = **$1.50**

7. It costs 4 times as much to outfit a football player as it does to outfit a basketball player. If it costs $260.00 to outfit a football player, how much more does it cost to outfit 10 football players than 10 basketball players?

65.   260.00   195.00
4)260.   − 65.00   x 10
        195.00   **$1,950.00**

Page 52

Answer Key

Something's Missing — I

Some story problems seem to be missing information. Often the information can be found in a Table of Measures. Use this Table of Measures to help solve the problems on this page.

12 inches = 1 foot   1,760 yards = 1 mile
36 inches = 1 yard   5,280 feet = 1 mile
1 yard = 3 feet

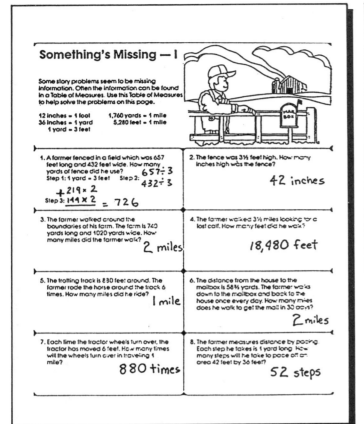

1. A farmer fenced in a field which was 657 feet long and 432 feet wide. How many yards of fence did he use?
Step 1: 1 yard = 3 feet   Step 2: $432 \div 3$
$657 \div 3$
219×2
Step 3: 144×2 = 726

2. The fence was 3½ feet high. How many inches high was the fence?
42 inches

3. The farmer walked around the boundaries of his farm. The farm is 740 yards long and 1020 yards wide. How many miles did the farmer walk?
2 miles

4. The farmer walked 3½ miles looking for a lost calf. How many feet did he walk?
18,480 feet

5. The trotting track is 880 feet around. The farmer rode the horse around the track 6 times. How many miles did he ride?
1 mile

6. The distance from the house to the mailbox is 58⅔ yards. The farmer walks down to the mailbox and back to the house once every day. How many miles does he walk to get the mail in 30 days?
2 miles

7. Each time the tractor wheels turn over, the tractor has moved 6 feet. How many times will the wheels turn over in traveling 1 mile?
880 times

8. The farmer measures distance by pacing. Each step he takes is 1 yard long. How many steps will he take to pace off an area 42 feet by 36 feet?
52 steps

Something's Missing — II

Use this Table of Measures to help solve the problems on this page.

100 centimeters (cm) = 1 meter (m)   10 decimeters (dm) = 1 meter (m)
1,000 meters (m) = 1 kilometer (km)   1,000 grams (g) = 1 kilogram (kg)

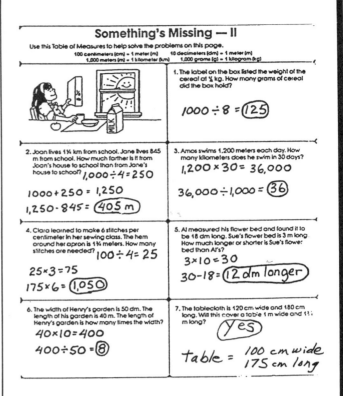

1. The label on the box listed the weight of the cereal at ⅛ kg. How many grams of cereal did the box hold?
$1000 \div 8 =$ (125)

2. Joan lives 1¼ km from school. Jane lives 845 m from school. How much farther is it from Joan's house to school than from Jane's house to school?
$1,000 \div 4 = 250$
$1000 + 250 = 1,250$
$1,250 - 845 =$ (405 m)

3. Amos swims 1,200 meters each day. How many kilometers does he swim in 30 days?
$1,200 \times 30 = 36,000$
$36,000 \div 1,000 =$ (36)

4. Clara learned to make 6 stitches per centimeter in her sewing class. The hem around her apron is 1¾ meters. How many stitches are needed?
$100 \div 4 = 25$
$25 \times 3 = 75$
$175 \times 6 =$ (1,050)

5. Al measured his flower bed and found it to be 18 dm long. Sue's flower bed is 3 m long. How much longer or shorter is Sue's flower bed than Al's?
$3 \times 10 = 30$
$30 - 18 =$ (12 dm longer)

6. The width of Henry's garden is 50 dm. The length of his garden is 40 m. The length of Henry's garden is how many times the width?
$40 \times 10 = 400$
$400 \div 50 =$ (8)

7. The tablecloth is 120 cm wide and 180 cm long. Will this cover a table 1 m wide and 1½ m long?
(Yes)
table = 100 cm wide
175 cm long

Something's Missing — III

Use this Table of Measures to help solve the problems on this page.

8 fluid ounces = 1 cup   2 pints = 1 quart   8 quarts = 1 peck   16 ounces = 1 pound
2 cups = 1 pint   4 quarts = 1 gallon   4 pecks = 1 bushel   2,000 pounds = 1 ton

1. The 5 pounds of hamburger needed for a cookout cost $5.60. How much does the hamburger cost per ounce?
step 1: 5) $\overline{5.60}$ 1.12
step 2: 1 pound = 16 ounces
step 3: 16) $\overline{1.12}$ = (7¢)

2. A new tractor weighs 1¼ tons. How many pounds does the tractor weigh?
$2000 \div 4 = 500$
$500 + 2,000 =$ (2,500)

3. A gallon of ice cream sells for $3.20. How much will a 1-cup serving of ice cream cost?
$2 \times 2 = 4$
$4 \times 4 = 16$
$3.20 \div 16 =$ (20¢)

4. 5 quarts of oil are needed for a car's oil change. How many oil changes can a mechanic make from a 50-gallon drum of oil?
$50 \times 4 = 200$
$200 \div 5 =$ (40)

5. Martha poured 24 cups of water into a jug. Her mother told her she needed 16 more cups of water to fill the jug. How many quarts will the jug hold?
$24 \div 4 = 6$
$16 \div 4 = 4$
$6 + 4 =$ (10)

6. A bushel of apples sells for $5.80. How much would a peck cost?
$5.80 \div 4 =$ ($1.45)

7. Bill sold a peck of strawberries at 85¢ a quart. How much money did he receive in all?
$.85 \times 8 =$ ($6.80)

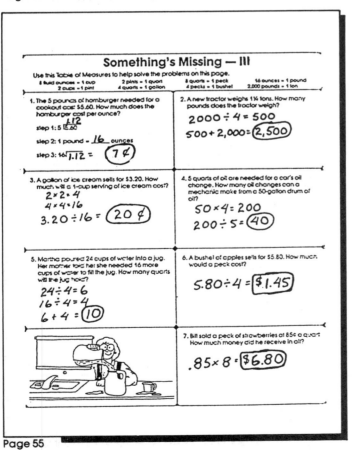

Something's Missing — IV

Some story problems seem to be missing information. Often the information can be found in a Table of Measures. Use this Table of Measures to help solve the problems on this page.

60 minutes = 1 hour   8 fluid ounces = 1 cup
24 hours = 1 day   1 dozen = 12
52 weeks = 1 year   16 ounces = 1 pound
2 cups = 1 pint
2 pints = 1 quart
4 quarts = 1 gallon

1. The clerk sold 5 dozen eggs for a total of $3.60. How much did each egg cost?
Step 1: 1 dozen = 12   Step 2: $5 \times 12 = 60$
Step 3: 60) $\overline{3.60}$ $.6$ 6¢

2. A 1-gallon jug will hold how many cups of cider?
16 cups

3. The clerk is paid $8.40 per hour. How much does he earn each minute he works?
14¢

4. A customer wanted 3¼ cups of syrup for a recipe. The syrup containers were marked in ounces. The clerk needed to look for a container which held how many ounces of syrup?
26 ounces

5. A 5-pound bag of sugar sells for $1.60. How much does each ounce of sugar cost?
2¢

6. The clerk has only 3 days of vacation left. How many minutes does he have before he has to go back to work?
4,320 minutes

7. A certain customer buys 1 pound of coffee every 2 weeks. How many pounds of coffee does this customer buy in one year?
26 pounds

8. One family buys 3 quarts of ice cream per week. How many cups of ice cream does this family eat each week?
12 cups

Answer Key

Too Much Information — I

Underline the distractor (unused fact) in each story and solve the problem.

1. Carl studied math for ¾ hour and then played with his dog for ½ hour before dinner. After dinner he studied 1½ hours for his other classes. How long altogether did Carl study?

$\frac{3}{4} = \frac{3}{4}$

$+1\frac{1}{2} = 1\frac{2}{4}$

$1\frac{5}{4} = \boxed{2\frac{1}{4}}$

2. Mr. Thomas teaches mathematics for 4½ hours each day, and then spends 2½ hours each day coaching the basketball team. How much time does he spend on basketball in 5 days?

$2\frac{1}{2} \times 5$

$\frac{5}{2} \times 5 = \frac{25}{2} = \boxed{12\frac{1}{2}}$

3. After school Maria spends ⅓ of her time practicing the piano, ¼ of her time on soccer practice and ⅙ of her time on voice lessons. What fraction of her time does Maria spend on music?

$\frac{1}{3} = \frac{2}{6}$

$+ \frac{1}{6} = \frac{1}{6}$

$\frac{3}{6} = \boxed{\frac{1}{2}}$

4. Mrs. Harper has 64 students in her choir. Of these students, ⅓ are boys. She also conducts the 48-member orchestra. How many music students does Mrs. Harper have in all?

$64 + 48 = \boxed{112}$

5. In one class of 24 students, 8 are in the band and 12 are involved in athletics. What fraction of the class is in the band?

$\frac{8}{24} = \boxed{\frac{1}{3}}$

6. Mr. Wood works for 6 hours cleaning up after each ball game. Altogether, there are 34 ball games. Mr. Wood is paid at the rate of $6.00 per hour. How many hours in all does Mr. Wood spend cleaning up after ball games?

$6 \times 34 = \boxed{204}$

7. A year is 365 days long. Students spend 180 days a year in school. Each school day is 6 hours long. How many hours do students spend in school each year?

$180 \times 6 = \boxed{1{,}080}$

Page 57

Too Much Information — II

Put a distractor in each of the following story problems and then solve the problems.

1. The pool is 12 feet wide and 25 feet long. Find the perimeter (distance around it).

Add: The pool is 6 feet deep

$12 + 25 = 37$

$37 \times 2 = \boxed{74 \text{ feet}}$

2. The pool is 25 feet long. How many laps (one length and back equals one lap) of the pool are equal to 100 yards?

Answers may vary for distractors.

$100 \times 3 = 300$

$300 \div 50 = \boxed{6}$

3. It takes 4 hours for all the water in the pool to go through the filter. In 24 hours, how many times has the water been filtered?

$24 \div 4 = \boxed{6}$

4. Ann swam 10 laps of the 25-foot-long pool in 5 minutes. How many feet per minute did Ann swim?

$10 \times 50 = 500$

$500 \div 5 = \boxed{100}$

5. Bill swam 1 mile (5,280 feet) in 15 minutes. How many feet per minute did Bill swim?

$5280 \div 15 = \boxed{352}$

6. Bill, Joe, Chuck and Don each swam 12 laps of the 25-foot-long pool. How far did they swim altogether?

$50 \times 12 = 600$

$600 \times 4 = \boxed{2{,}400 \text{ feet}}$

7. Mr. Long pays Bill $3.50 each day to clean the pool and check the chemicals. How much will Bill earn if the pool is open 110 days this summer?

$3.50 \times 110 = \boxed{\$385.00}$

Page 58

Too Much Information — III

Underline the distractor (unused fact) in each story and solve the problem.

1. Bill is the sports writer for the school paper. He is allowed to use 2 pages for his articles. There are 32 lines of type on each page. The editorial section is 1 page long. The average line contains 16 words. How many words are there in Bill's sports section?

1,024 words

2. Bill wrote an article on basketball which took 12 lines. He wrote an article on intramural sports which took 14 lines. The average line contains 16 words. How many words were there in the basketball article?

192 words

3. Each page has 32 lines of type and 16 words per line. On one page Bill had an article covering 8 lines, using 128 words, and another article covering 11 lines. The rest of this page was to be used for a fan appreciation article. How many words could he use in the fan appreciation article?

208 words

4. Last week Bill attended 3 basketball games which each lasted 2 hours and 15 minutes. He averaged 28 minutes in writing about each of these events. How much time altogether did Bill spend attending sports events?

6 hrs. 45 min.

5. Bill spends 3 hours every school day attending sporting events and writing them up for the paper. He attends school from 8:00 a.m. until 3:00 p.m. How much time each week does Bill spend on his sports writing job?

15 hrs.

6. The school paper has a staff of 12 people. Each time the paper is published, 14 spaces of advertising are sold for $7.50 each. How much is collected in a semester for advertising if the paper is published 12 times per semester?

$1,260.00

7. Subscriptions to the paper sell for $2.50 for the 12 issues. Papers are sold at newsstands for 25¢ each. 430 subscriptions will bring in how much money?

$1,075.00

8. The school paper staff was honored with a banquet. Besides the 12-member student staff, 134 adults attended. Banquet tickets cost $14.00 each. How much did the adults pay in all?

$1,876.00

Page 59

Too Much Information — IV

Put a distractor in each of the following problems and then solve the problem.

1. Mr. Johns is placing stepping-stones across his garden. Each stepping-stone costs $1.25.
The stones will be placed 6 inches apart. (distractor)
How much will 12 stones cost?

$15.00

2. Mr. Johns bought a garden tractor for $564.00 and used it for 12 years. Answers may vary for distractors.
How much did each year of use cost?

$47.00

3. The 14 flowering shrubs for Mr. Johns's garden cost $9.60 each. ______
How much did the shrubs cost altogether?

$134.40

4. Putting an ornamental fence around the garden, which is 37 feet long and 27 feet wide, will cost $18.00 for each 4-foot section. ______
How much will the fence cost?

$576.00

5. It took 2 children 14 hours to paint the fence. Mr. Johns paid them each $3.25 per hour. ______
How much altogether did he pay the fence painters?

$91.00

6. For his garden, Mr. Johns bought a picnic table for $42.95, 4 benches at $14.49 each, and 6 chairs at $12.25 each. ______
How much did he spend altogether?

$174.41

7. A charcoal grill cost $19.95. It cost Mr. Johns $112.00 to build a brick enclosure for it. ______
How much did the grill and the enclosure cost altogether?

$131.95

8. Mr. Johns bought a bug light for $28.95 and 3 cans of insect spray that cost $4.35 each. ______
How much did Mr. Johns spend on insect control?

$42.00

Page 60

Answer Key

Too Much or Not Enough? — I

Each of the following problems contains too much or too little information. If too much information is given, underline the distractor and solve the problem. If not enough information is given, write "NE."

1. Chuck has 6 rows across the garden for every 5 feet of space. How many rows in all are in his garden?

$$NE$$

2. Chuck has 3 times as many rows of beans as peas, and he has 4 times as many rows of potatoes as peas. He has 3 rows of peas. How many rows of beans are there in Chuck's garden?

$$3 \times 3 = \boxed{9}$$

3. Cucumber plants produced an average of 18 cucumbers per hill. 5 of the cucumbers weighed one pound each. There were 12 hills altogether. How many cucumbers were produced in all?

$$18 \times 12 = \boxed{216}$$

4. Chuck had 49 potato plants. The average potato weighed 1¼ pounds. How much did the potatoes weigh altogether?

$$NE$$

5. Chuck paid Bill $3.50 per hour to help him in his garden. Bill dug potatoes for 7 hours and picked beans for 1½ hours. How much did Chuck pay Bill to dig potatoes?

$$\$3.50 \times 7 = \boxed{\$24.50}$$

6. Potatoes sell for $2.79 per 10-pound bag. Chuck bagged potatoes for 6 hours. How much money did he make?

$$NE$$

7. Chuck sold $4.50 worth of green beans and $2.70 worth of tomatoes. At 30¢ per pound, how many pounds of green beans did Chuck sell?

$$\$4.50 \div .30 = \boxed{15}$$

Too Much or Not Enough? — II

Each of the following problems contains too much or too little information. If too much information is given, underline the distractor and solve the problem. If not enough information is given, write "NE."

1. An Earth day is 24 hours long. A day on Mars is equal to 25 Earth hours, while a day on Mercury is equal to 2,100 Earth hours. How many times as long as a day on Mars is a day on Mercury?

$$2100 \div 25 = \boxed{84}$$

2. A year on Earth is 365 days long. A year on Mercury is equal to 88 Earth days. A year on Pluto is equal to 248 Earth years. How many more Earth days are there in an Earth year than in a Mercury year?

$$365 - 88 = \boxed{277}$$

3. A day on Earth is 24 hours long. A Uranus day is shorter than an Earth day. How many hours are there in a Uranus year?

$$NE$$

4. An Earth day is 24 hours long. A Pluto day is equal to 248 Earth years. How many Earth hours less is 30 days on Earth than 7 days on Pluto?

$$30 \times 24 = 720 \quad 980$$
$$140 \times 7 = 980 \quad -720$$
$$\boxed{260}$$

5. Venus's day is equal to 5,400 Earth hours. An Earth year is 365 days long. An Earth day is 24 hours long. A Venus day is how many times as long as an Earth day?

$$5,400 \div 24 = \boxed{225}$$

6. An Earth day is 24 hours long. A Mercury day is equal to 2,100 Earth hours. A Pluto day is equal to 140 Earth hours. A Mercury day is how many times as long as a Pluto day?

$$2100 \div 140 = \boxed{15}$$

7. An Earth day is 24 hours long. A day on Saturn is equal to 10 Earth hours. A Mars day is how many times as long as a day on Saturn?

$$NE$$

Too Much or Not Enough? — III

Each of the following problems contains too much or too little information. If too much information is given, underline the distractor and solve the problem. If not enough information is given, write "NE."

1. The 28 students in the 6th grade went on a picnic. They took 72 sandwiches, 56 soft drinks and 96 cookies. 4 of the boys ate ¼ of the cookies. How many cookies were left for each of the other students?

72 cookies left, 3 for each student.

2. One of the girls baked half of the cookies. Two boys baked the rest of the cookies. The girl who baked half the cookies spent $5.00 on ingredients. How much did she spend on flour?

$$NE$$

3. The 56 soft drinks cost 22¢ each. The sandwiches cost 85¢ each to make. How much was each of the 28 students' share of the soft drink cost?

44¢

4. If the sandwiches had been bought at a deli, the cost for each sandwich would have been 3 times the cost for making each sandwich at home. How much would 72 sandwiches cost at the deli?

$$NE$$

5. The students drank 75% of the 56 soft drinks and ate ¾ of the 72 sandwiches. How many sandwiches were left uneaten?

12

6. The school is ¾ mile from the park. The 16 students whose parents did not pick them up at the park walked home. How far altogether did these students walk?

$$NE$$

7. Of the 28 students, 1 student did not enjoy the picnic. Of the rest of the class, ⅔ want to have another picnic soon. 2 students said they enjoyed it, but did not want another picnic for a while. How many students want another picnic soon?

18

8. Of the 28 students, all but 4 live in town. ⅞ of those living in town walk to school. Some students ride their bikes to school. How many students are brought to school by their parents?

$$NE$$

Too Much or Not Enough? — IV

Each of the following problems contains too much or too little information. If too much information is given, underline the distractor and solve the problem. If not enough information is given, write "NE."

1. The local high school has won 85% of its basketball games and 60% of its football games over the last 10 years. How many of the school's 220 basketball games has it won?

187

2. The wrestling team has won ¾ of its 28 matches over the last 2 years and the football team has won 70% of its games over the last 2 years. How many games did the football team win?

$$NE$$

3. There are 8 members on the tennis team. There are 3 times as many basketball players as tennis players. 3 times as many students play football as play basketball, and 1½ times as many students play baseball as play basketball. Altogether, how many students play basketball and baseball?

60

4. The boys' basketball team has won 340 more games than it has lost over the last 20 years. What percentage of its games has the team won?

$$NE$$

5. The gym seats 4,500 fans. The first game of the season was sold out. For the last game of the season there were 1,250 empty seats. Tickets for adults cost $2.50 each. Student tickets cost $1.25 each. How much money was collected for the first game of the season if 2,200 of the fans were students?

$8,500.00

6. The wrestling team had 127 fans who each paid $1.50 to attend the first meet. 246 people each paid $1.50 to see the last meet. How much money was collected at the last meet?

$369.00

7. The total attendance for the 5 home football games was 33,000. The total attendance for the 89 home wrestling meets was 1,650. What was the average attendance at each of the football games?

6,600

8. Of the school's 180 athletes, ⅓ plan to attend college. Of the entire student body, 40% plan to attend college. How many of the athletes plan to go to college?

120

    118   IF8747 Math Topics

Answer Key

Write Your Own Problem

Solve each problem. Then write a new question for each one so that you have a different story problem and solve your own problem.

1. A building contractor pays a carpenter $12.00 per hour and a carpenter's helper $8.00 per hour. In a 40-hour week, how much does the contractor pay the carpenter and his helper altogether?
   Solution:
   New Question: $800.00
   In a 40-hour week, how much does the carpenter's helper earn?
   New Solution: $320.00

2. Last year the contractor paid $124,800.00 in wages to his employees. ⅗ of the wages went to the carpenters. The rest of the wages went to the carpenters' helpers. How much altogether were the carpenters paid last year?
   Solution: $74,880.00
   New Question:
   New Solution: Answers may vary.

3. The contractor was paid $340,000.00 to build a commercial building. He paid $31,200.00 to his employees in wages, $920.00 for employee fringe benefits, $1,800.00 for office costs and $210,000.00 for materials. How much profit did he make off of this job?
   Solution: $96,080.00
   New Question:
   New Solution: Answers may vary.

4. A garage was built in 4 workdays of 8 hours each by 2 carpenters and 1 helper. The carpenters were each paid $12.00 per hour, and the helper was paid $8.00 per hour. How much in wages did building this garage cost?
   Solution: $1,024.00
   New Question:
   New Solution: Answers may vary.

5. Last year the contractor built and sold 23 houses for a total profit of $183,000.00. However, he built 7 more houses which sold at a loss of $4,300.00 each. What was his overall profit from building houses?
   Solution: $152,900.00
   New Question:
   New Solution: Answers may vary.

6. Altogether, the contractor made a profit of $243,000.00 last year. He gave $27,000.00 to local charities and $24,300.00 to a church. How much more than 15% of his profit did he give away?
   Solution: $14,850.00
   New Question:
   New Solution: Answers may vary.

Page 65

You Can Do It! — I

Solve the following problems.

1. The school is ⅝ mile from Jack's house. How many miles does Jack ride his bike to and from school in 5 days?
   $5 \times \frac{5}{8} = \frac{25}{8} \times \frac{2}{1} = \frac{50}{8} =$ (6¼)

2. The library is 2¼ miles farther from Jack's house than the school is. The school is ⅝ mile away. How far does Jack live from the library?
   $2\frac{1}{4} = 2\frac{2}{8}$
   $+ \frac{5}{8} = \frac{5}{8}$
   (2⅞ miles)

3. The library is 2¼ miles from Jack's house. The ice cream parlor is ½ mile farther down the street. How far has he pedaled his bike if he goes to the library, then to the ice cream parlor, and then back home?
   $2\frac{1}{4} = 2\frac{1}{4}$
   $+ \frac{1}{2} = \frac{2}{4}$
   $2\ \frac{3}{4}$
   $2\frac{3}{4} \times 2 =$ (5½ miles)

4. Jack lives 12 miles from the ball park. He can pedal his bike 10 miles in 30 minutes. How long will it take Jack to ride his bike to the ball park?
   $30 \div 10 = 3$
   $12 \times 3 =$ (36 min.)

5. It takes 4 trips around the track to make a mile. Jack pedaled his bike around the track 24 times. It took him 30 minutes. How many miles per hour was Jack pedaling?
   $24 \div 4 = 6$
   $6 \times 2 =$ (12)

6. It takes Jack 15 minutes to walk a mile. It takes Jack 4 minutes to ride his bike a mile. How much farther can he ride his bike than he can walk in one hour?
   $60 \div 4 = 15$
   $60 \div 15 = 4$
   $15 - 4 =$ (11 miles)

7. Jack rode his bike for 2⅓ hours at a speed of 12 miles per hour. The next 1½ hours his speed dropped to 10 miles per hour. How many miles did he cover altogether?
   $2\frac{1}{3} \times 12 = 28$
   $1\frac{1}{2} \times 10 = 15$
   $28 + 15 =$ (43)

Page 66

You Can Do It! — I

Solve the following problems.

1. The club has 120 members. It costs each member $200.00 to join, and the annual dues are $60.00 per member. How much is collected in dues each year?
   $120 \times 60.00 =$ ($7,200.00)

2. Dinner at the club costs $12.00 per person. Lunch at the club costs $4.00 per person. If a member ate dinner at the club 38 times during one year, how much would these dinners cost in all?
   $12.00 \times 38 =$ ($456.00)

3. The dining room at the club is 38 feet long and 22 feet wide. 96 diners can be seated at one time. If ¾ of the 120 members come to dinner and each brings a guest, how many must wait for the 2nd seating?
   $120 \times \frac{3}{4} = 90$
   $90 \times 2 = 180$
   $180 - 96 =$ (84)

4. If 96 members eat dinners that cost $12.00 each, how much in all will these dinners cost?
   $12.00 \times 96 =$ ($1,152.00)

5. One day ¼ of the 120 members ate the $4.00 lunch and ½ of the 120 members ate the $12.00 dinner. Altogether, how much more was spent for dinner than for lunch?
   $\frac{1}{4} \times 120 = 30$
   $30 \times 4 = 120.$
   $\frac{1}{2} \times 120 = 60$
   $60 \times 12 = 720.$
   $720 - 120 =$ ($600.00)

6. The annual Halloween party is free for members wearing costumes. A $5.00 admission fee is charged those not in costume. ⅕ of the 120 members were not in costume. Altogether, how much did these members pay?
   $\frac{1}{5} \times 120 = 24$
   $24 \times 5.00 =$ ($120.00)

7. A $25.00 per person admission is charged for the Christmas party, and the money is used to buy gifts for children. Members and guests attending the party totaled 180. How much money was collected?
   $180 \times 25.00 =$ ($4,500.00)

Page 67

You Can Do It! — III

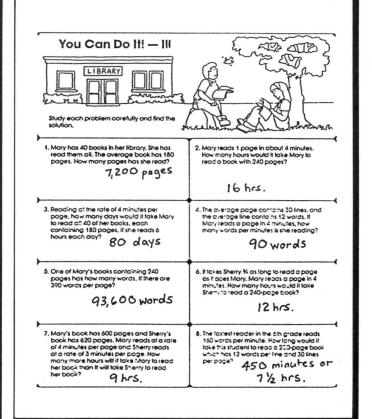

Study each problem carefully and find the solution.

1. Mary has 40 books in her library. She has read them all. The average book has 180 pages. How many pages has she read?
   7,200 pages

2. Mary reads 1 page in about 4 minutes. How many hours would it take Mary to read a book with 240 pages?
   16 hrs.

3. Reading at the rate of 4 minutes per page, how many days would it take Mary to read all 40 of her books, each containing 180 pages, if she reads 6 hours each day?
   80 days

4. The average page contains 30 lines, and the average line contains 12 words. If Mary reads a page in 4 minutes, how many words per minutes is she reading?
   90 words

5. One of Mary's books containing 240 pages has how many words, if there are 390 words per page?
   93,600 words

6. It takes Sherry ¾ as long to read a page as it does Mary. Mary reads a page in 4 minutes. How many hours would it take Sherry to read a 240-page book?
   12 hrs.

7. Mary's book has 600 pages and Sherry's book has 620 pages. Mary reads at a rate of 4 minutes per page and Sherry reads at a rate of 3 minutes per page. How many more hours will it take Mary to read her book than it will take Sherry to read her book?
   9 hrs.

8. The fastest reader in the 6th grade reads 160 words per minute. How long would it take this student to read a 200-page book which has 12 words per line and 30 lines per page?
   450 minutes or 7½ hrs.

Page 68

Answer Key

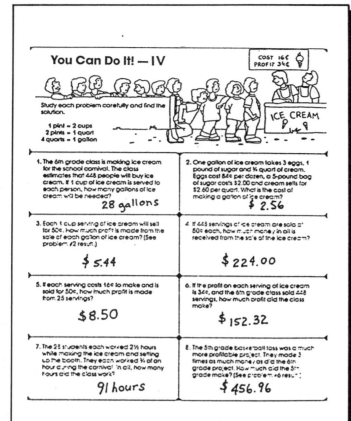

You Can Do It! — IV

COST 16¢ PROFIT 34¢

Study each problem carefully and find the solution.

1 pint = 2 cups
2 pints = 1 quart
4 quarts = 1 gallon

1. The 6th grade class is making ice cream for the school carnival. The class estimates that 448 people will buy ice cream. If 1 cup of ice cream is served to each person, how many gallons of ice cream will be needed?

28 gallons

2. One gallon of ice cream takes 3 eggs, 1 pound of sugar and ¾ quart of cream. Eggs cost 84¢ per dozen, a 5-pound bag of sugar costs $2.00 and cream sells for $2.60 per quart. What is the cost of making a gallon of ice cream?

$ 2.56

3. Each 1 cup serving of ice cream will sell for 50¢. How much profit is made from the sale of each gallon of ice cream? (See problem #2 result.)

$ 5.44

4. If 448 servings of ice cream are sold at 50¢ each, how much money is received from the sale of the ice cream?

$ 224.00

5. If each serving costs 16¢ to make and is sold for 50¢, how much profit is made from 25 servings?

$ 8.50

6. If the profit on each serving of ice cream is 34¢, and the 6th grade class sold 448 servings, how much profit did the class make?

$ 152.32

7. The 28 students each worked 2½ hours while making the ice cream and setting up the booth. They each worked ¾ of an hour during the carnival. In all, how many hours did the class work?

91 hours

8. The 5th grade basketball toss was a much more profitable project. They made 3 times as much money as did the 6th grade project. How much did the 5th grade make? (See problem #6 result.)

$ 456.96

Page 69

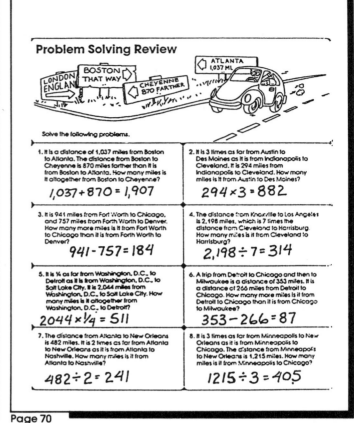

Problem Solving Review

ATLANTA 1,037 ML **LONDON ENGLAND** **BOSTON THAT WAY** **CHEYENNE 870 FARTHER**

Solve the following problems.

1. It is a distance of 1,037 miles from Boston to Atlanta. The distance from Boston to Cheyenne is 870 miles farther than it is from Boston to Atlanta. How many miles is it altogether from Boston to Cheyenne?

1,037 + 870 = 1,907

2. It is 3 times as far from Austin to Des Moines as it is from Indianapolis to Cleveland. It is 294 miles from Indianapolis to Cleveland. How many miles is it from Austin to Des Moines?

294 × 3 = 882

3. It is 941 miles from Fort Worth to Chicago, and 757 miles from Forth Worth to Denver. How many more miles is it from Fort Worth to Chicago than it is from Forth Worth to Denver?

941 − 757 = 184

4. The distance from Knoxville to Los Angeles is 2,198 miles, which is 7 times the distance from Cleveland to Harrisburg. How many miles is it from Cleveland to Harrisburg?

2,198 ÷ 7 = 314

5. It is ¼ as far from Washington, D.C., to Detroit as it is from Washington, D.C., to Salt Lake City. It is 2,044 miles from Washington, D.C., to Salt Lake City. How many miles is it altogether from Washington, D.C., to Detroit?

2044 × ¼ = 511

6. A trip from Detroit to Chicago and then to Milwaukee is a distance of 353 miles. It is a distance of 266 miles from Detroit to Chicago. How many more miles is it from Detroit to Chicago than it is from Chicago to Milwaukee?

353 − 266 = 87

7. The distance from Atlanta to New Orleans is 482 miles. It is 2 times as far from Atlanta to Nashville. How many miles is it from Atlanta to Nashville?

482 ÷ 2 = 241

8. It is 3 times as far from Minneapolis to New Orleans as it is from Minneapolis to Chicago. The distance from Minneapolis to New Orleans is 1,215 miles. How many miles is it from Minneapolis to Chicago?

1215 ÷ 3 = 405

Page 70

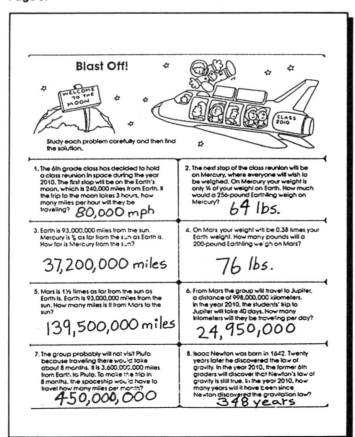

Blast Off!

WELCOME TO THE MOON **CLASS 2010**

Study each problem carefully and then find the solution.

1. The 6th grade class has decided to hold a class reunion in space during the year 2010. The first stop will be on the Earth's moon, which is 240,000 miles from Earth. If the trip to the moon takes 3 hours, how many miles per hour will they be traveling?

80,000 mph

2. The next stop of the class reunion will be on Mercury, where everyone will wish to be weighed. On Mercury your weight is only ¼ of your weight on Earth. How much would a 256-pound Earthling weigh on Mercury?

64 lbs.

3. Earth is 93,000,000 miles from the sun. Mercury is ⅖ as far from the sun as Earth is. How far is Mercury from the sun?

37,200,000 miles

4. On Mars your weight will be 0.38 times your Earth weight. How many pounds will a 200-pound Earthling weigh on Mars?

76 lbs.

5. Mars is 1½ times as far from the sun as Earth is. Earth is 93,000,000 miles from the sun. How many miles is it from Mars to the sun?

139,500,000 miles

6. From Mars the group will travel to Jupiter, a distance of 998,000,000 kilometers. In the year 2010, the students' trip to Jupiter will take 40 days. How many kilometers will they be traveling per day?

24,950,000

7. The group probably will not visit Pluto because traveling there would take about 8 months. It is 3,600,000,000 miles from Earth to Pluto. To make the trip in 8 months, the spaceship would have to travel how many miles per month?

450,000,000

8. Isaac Newton was born in 1642. Twenty years later he discovered the law of gravity. In the year 2010, the former 6th graders will discover that Newton's law of gravity is still true. In the year 2010, how many years will it have been since Newton discovered the gravitation law?

348 years

Page 71

Mean Monster's Way-out Weigh-in

Name _____

Mean Monster is a fifth grader who plays football for the OID-DOIG OUTLAWS. He now weighs 519 pounds and stands 7 feet 5 inches tall. He has only three teeth left, and his nose has been broken four times. He has some trouble in school. Can you help him figure out these math problems?

Work the problems on another paper.   Answer Space

1.	519 − 338 = 181 lbs.
2.	519 + 338 = 857 lbs.
3.	192 ÷ 16 = 12 lbs.
4.	7 × 16 = 112 oz.
5.	519 − 463 = 56 lbs.
6.	519 + 463 + 338 = 1,320 lbs.
7.	519 × 3 = 1,557 lbs.
8.	256 ÷ 16 = 16 lbs.
9.	519 × 16 = 8,304 oz.
10.	519 − 73 = 446 lbs.

Page 72

Answer Key

Buggs I. Lyke Serves Lunch

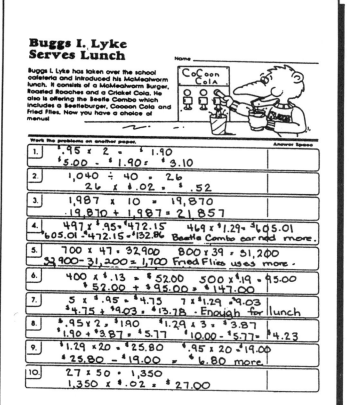

Buggs I. Lyke has taken over the school cafeteria and introduced his McMealworm lunch. It consists of a McMealworm Burger, Roasted Roaches and a Cricket Cola. He also is offering the Beetle Combo which includes a Beetleburger, Cocoon Cola and Fried Flies. Now you have a choice of menus!

Name _____

Work the problems on another paper.   Answer Space

1. $.95 × 2 = $1.90
   $5.00 - $1.90 = $3.10

2. 1,040 ÷ 40 = 26
   26 × $.02 = $.52

3. 1,987 × 10 = 19,870
   19,870 + 1,987 = 21,857

4. 497 × $.95 = $472.15   469 × $1.29 = $605.01
   $605.01 - $472.15 = $132.86 Beetle Combo earned more.

5. 700 × 47 = 32,900   800 × 39 = 31,200
   32,900 - 31,200 = 1,700 Fried Flies was used more.

6. 400 × $.13 = $52.00   500 × $.19 = $95.00
   $52.00 + $95.00 = $147.00

7. 5 × $.95 = $4.75   7 × $1.29 = $9.03
   $4.75 + $9.03 = $13.78 - Enough for lunch

8. $.95 × 2 = $1.90 $1.29 × 3 = $3.87
   $1.90 + $3.87 = $5.77 $10.00 - $5.77 = $4.23

9. $1.29 × 20 = $25.80 $.95 × 20 = $19.00
   $25.80 - $19.00 = $6.80 more.

10. 27 × 50 = 1,350
    1,350 × $.02 = $27.00

Page 73

Shifty Sam's "Rip-Off" Record Shop

Shifty Sam sells the latest rock releases along with some oldies that go clear back to when your teachers were teenagers. You have to keep a close eye on Sam, however, or you may get ripped off.

Name _____

Work the problems on another paper.   Answer Space

1. $8.98 × 5 = $44.90
   $46.95 - $44.90 = $2.05 more on sale

2. $4,540.90 ÷ 455 = $9.98 - (Sam charged)
   $9.98 - $7.99 = $1.99 extra for each record

3. $4.59 - $3.29 = $1.30
   323 × $1.30 = $419.90 extra

4. 4,000 × $1.77 = $7,080 more

5. 298 × $9.09 = 2,708.82 total sales
   $9.09 - $3.67 = $5.42   298 × $5.42 = $1,615.16 profit

6. $3.67 × 12 = $44.04
   $44.04 - $44.00 = .04 She will save.

7. 180 × $.79 = $142.20 $200 - 142.20 = $57.80
   $57.80 - $47.80 = $10.00 Sam cheated you.

8. 7,000 × $3.99 = $27,930 total sales
   7,000 × $2.00 = $14,000 profit

9. 3,500 × $1.79 = $6,265.00 extra

10. 4,328 × $4.99 = $21,596.72 total sales
    4,328 × $1.45 = $6,275.60 profit

Page 74

Smelly Belly Knows Your Nose

Smelly Belly wants to capture the perfume market at your school. She has an exquisite nose for delicate scents and delightful fragrances which she bottles and sells to the students.

Name _____

Work the problems on another paper.   Answer Space

1. 385 × $7.99 = $3,076.15

2. $533.61 ÷ 49 = $10.89

3. $987.34 + $1,278.43 = $2,265.77

4. 298 × $6.39 = $1,904.22

5. $1,765.01 - $657.57 = $1,107.44

6. 98 × $11.85 = $1,161.30

7. $930.92 ÷ 68 = $13.69

8. $3,642.03 ÷ $9.87 = 369

9. $736.77 ÷ 123 = $5.99

10. $4,789.01 - $2,997.43 = $1,791.58

Page 75

Booming Business at Pat's Pets Aplenty

Pat wants to put "A Pet in Every Home," so he is having a gigantic sale on all of his wonderful pets.

Name _____

Work the problems on another paper.   Answer Space

1. $2.99 × 18 = $53.82

2. $2.39 + $8.67 = $11.06

3. $.84 ÷ 12 = $.07

4. $20.00 - $4.79 = $15.21

5. $13.45 - $9.99 = $3.46

6. $23.40 ÷ 60 = $.39

7. $1.41 × 40 = $56.40

8. $2.99 × 10 = $29.90

9. $2.39 + $3.13 = $5.52

10. $41.04 ÷ 19 = $2.16

Page 76

Answer Key

Shifty Sam's Sale

Shifty Sam sells almost anything you would want to buy. Shifty is having a sale, and he says he's almost giving things away. But be careful. Compare his sale prices with his regular prices before you decide to buy.

Work the problems on another paper.   Answer Space

1. ① $1.39 + $1.45 = $2.84
   ② $2.89 - $2.84 = $.05   Lose

2. ① $7.99 + 8.79 = 16.78
   ② 16.89 - 16.78 = $.11 - Lose

3. ① $.98 + $2.87 = $3.85
   ② 3.85 - 3.50 = .35   Save

4. ① $34.57 + $45.99 = $80.56
   ② 89.95 - 80.56 = $9.39   Lose

5. ① $167.98 + $155.89 = $323.87
   ② $323.87 - $323.85 = $ .02   Save

6. ① $2.39 + $1.99 = $4.38
   ② $4.38 - $3.99 = $ .39   Save

7. ① $39.67 + $19.98 = $59.65
   ② $59.65 - $49.99 = $9.66   Save

8. ① $1.78 + $1.98 = $3.76
   ② $3.76 - $3.75 = $ .01   Save

9. ① $33.99 + $37.88 = $71.87
   ② $71.87 - $70.00 = $1.87   Save

10. ① $7.99 + $24.99 = $32.98
    ② $33.50 - $32.98 = $ .52   Lose

Page 77

Something's Fishy at Pat's Pet Shop

Pat has received a gigantic shipment of fish at his pet shop for his "Love A Fish Sale." Help him figure out how much money he could make.

Work the problems on another paper.   Answer Space

1. ① 1,750 ÷ 10 = 175
   ② 175 x $1.00 = $175.00

2. ① 324 ÷ 6 = 54
   ② 54 x $3.25 = $175.50

3. ① 648 ÷ 12 = 54
   ② 54 x $1.00 = $54.00

4. ① 371 ÷ 7 = 53
   ② 53 x .99 = $52.47

5. ① 675 ÷ 25 = 27
   ② 27 x 2 = $54.00

6. ① 1,281 ÷ 21 = 61
   ② 61 x $4.99 = $304.39

7. ① 900 ÷ 25 = 36
   ② 36 x $3.00 = $108.00

8. ① 253 ÷ 11 = 23
   ② 23 x $1.99 = $45.77

9. ① 168 ÷ 3 = 56
   ② 56 x $2.99 = $167.44

10. ① 1,452 ÷ 33 = 44
    ② 44 x $6.79 = $298.76

Page 78

Snails in a Pail

Sly Me Slugg, world-famous French chef, has made his last food business, Snails in a Pail, the most popular restaurant in the whole area. This is his menu:

Slime Soup $.49
Slugburgers $1.69
Chicken-Fried Snails $2.99
Slimy Slush $.89
Snailcream Shakes $1.49
Snailbits Salad $1.09

Work the problems on another paper.   Answer Space

1. $.89 x 60 = $53.40 $1.49 x 40 = $59.60
   $53.40 + $59.60 = $113.00

2. $1.69 x 15 = $25.35
   $40.00 - $25.35 = $14.65

3. $.49 + 1.69 + 2.99 + .89 + 1.49 + 1.09 = $8.64
   $10.00 - $8.64 = $1.36

4. $43.61 + $38.22 = $81.83
   $81.83 ÷ .49 = 167

5. (1.69 x 9 = 15.21) + (2.99 x 3 = 8.97) + (1.09 x 2 = 2.18)
   + (1.49 x 5 = 7.45) + (.89 x 10 = 8.90) = $42.71

6. $1.69 x 200 = $338 $2.99 x 79 = $236.21
   $338 + $236.21 = $574.21

7. 1.69 x 10 = $16.90   1.49 x 10 = $14.90   .89 x 10 = $8.90
   $16.90 + $14.90 + $8.90 = $40.70

8. $1,252 + $1,765 + $2,998 = $6,015
   $6,015 ÷ 3 = $2,005

9. (.49 x 8 = 3.92) + (2.99 x 12 = 35.88) + (1.69 x 4 = 6.76)
   + (.89 x 10 = 8.90) = $55.46

10. $161.46 ÷ $2.99 = 54   Chicken-Fried Snails
    $116.22 ÷ $1.49 = 78   Snailcream Shakes

Page 79

Big Bucks for You!

Your book, *The Secret Life of a Teenage Dracula*, earns you a nice bit of money in royalties. (A royalty is the publisher's payment to you as author of the book.) You need a checking account to keep the money in while you find ways to spend your new wealth.

Use the information on the next page and compute your payments, deposits and balance on the checkbook record below.

Problem Number	Transaction	Payment	Deposit	Balance
1	Deposit (Royalty Check)		$1000.00	$1000.00
1	Record Store	234.56		765.44
2	Pizza Shop	47.76		717.68
3	Clothing Shop	389.99		327.69
4	Deposit		1,712.34	2,040.03
5	Bicycle Shop	667.09		1,372.94
5	Perfume	37.89		1,335.05
6	Sports Store	203.45		1,131.60
7	Snails in a Pail	56.17		1,075.43
8	Health Club	150.90		924.53
9	Deposit		4,451.01	5,375.54
10	Football Game	4,339.98		1,035.56
11	Radio Store	198.79		836.77
12	Friendly loan	500.00		336.77
13	Deposit		456.78	793.55
14	Phone Bill	793.55		0

Page 80

Answer Key

Page 81

Use with page 80.

Work the problems on another paper. $88 Balancing a checkbook   Answer Space

1. $0 + $1,000.00 = $1,000.00
   $1,000.00 - $234.56 = $765.44

2. $765.44 - $47.76 = $717.68

3. $717.68 - $389.99 = $327.69

4. $327.69 + $1,712.34 = $2,040.03
   $2,040.03 - $667.09 = $1,372.94

5. $1,372.94 - $37.89 = $1,335.05

6. $1,335.05 - $203.45 = $1,131.60

7. $1,131.60 - $56.17 = $1,075.43

8. $1,075.43 - $150.90 = $924.53

9. $924.53 + $4,451.01 = $5,375.54

10. $5,375.54 - $4,339.98 = $1,035.56

11. $1,035.56 - $198.79 = $836.77

12. $836.77 - $500.00 = $336.77

13. $336.77 + $456.78 = $793.55

14. $793.55 - $793.55 = $0

Page 82

Hairy Spiders and Mighty Mites

Name _____

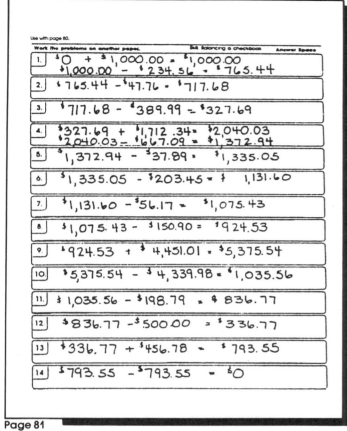

Work the problems on another paper.   Answer Space

1. $\frac{3}{8}$ in. - $\frac{4}{16}$ in. = $\frac{6}{16}$ in. - $\frac{4}{16}$ in. = $\frac{2}{16}$ in. = $\frac{1}{8}$ in.

2. $\frac{3}{4}$ in. - $\frac{1}{2}$ in. = $\frac{3}{4}$ in. - $\frac{2}{4}$ in. = $\frac{1}{4}$ in.

3. $\frac{11}{12}$ in. - $\frac{1}{4}$ in. = $\frac{11}{12}$ in. - $\frac{3}{12}$ in. = $\frac{8}{12}$ in. = $\frac{2}{3}$ in.

4. $\frac{5}{8}$ in. + $\frac{1}{2}$ in. = $\frac{5}{8}$ in. + $\frac{4}{8}$ in. = $\frac{9}{8}$ in. = 1$\frac{1}{8}$ in.

5. $\frac{2}{3}$ in. + $\frac{7}{8}$ in. = $\frac{16}{24}$ in. + $\frac{21}{24}$ in. = $\frac{37}{24}$ in. = 1$\frac{13}{24}$ in.

6. $\frac{1}{4}$ in. + $\frac{1}{3}$ in. = $\frac{3}{12}$ in. + $\frac{4}{12}$ in. = $\frac{7}{12}$ in.

7. $\frac{9}{12}$ in. - $\frac{1}{8}$ in. = $\frac{6}{24}$ in. - $\frac{3}{24}$ in. = $\frac{3}{24}$ in. = $\frac{1}{8}$ in.

8. $\frac{1}{8}$ in. - $\frac{1}{32}$ in. = $\frac{4}{32}$ in. - $\frac{1}{32}$ in. = $\frac{3}{32}$ in.

9. $\frac{3}{4}$ in. - $\frac{1}{12}$ in. = $\frac{9}{12}$ in. - $\frac{6}{12}$ in. = $\frac{3}{12}$ in. = $\frac{1}{4}$ in.

10. $\frac{1}{2}$ in. + $\frac{1}{12}$ in. = $\frac{6}{12}$ in. + $\frac{1}{12}$ in. = $\frac{7}{12}$ in.

Page 83

Sam Sillicook's Secret Recipe!

Name _____

Sam Sillicook, world famous pizza maker, has just published his super secret recipe for The Tongue Blaster Pizza. This is the recipe:

1/4 cup of Tabasco sauce   3/8 cup of mustard
1/3 cup of red onions   2/7 cup of chili pepper
2/5 cup of horseradish   2/9 cup of garlic
1/6 cup of cayenne pepper

Serves 6 hungry people

Work the problems on another paper.

1.
$\frac{1}{3}$ × $\frac{1}{4}$ = $\frac{1}{12}$ c. Tabasco
$\frac{1}{3}$ × $\frac{1}{3}$ = $\frac{1}{9}$ c. red onions
$\frac{1}{3}$ × $\frac{2}{5}$ = $\frac{2}{15}$ c. horseradish
$\frac{1}{3}$ × $\frac{1}{6}$ = $\frac{1}{18}$ c. cayenne
$\frac{1}{3}$ × $\frac{3}{8}$ = $\frac{3}{8}$ c. mustard
$\frac{1}{3}$ × $\frac{2}{7}$ = $\frac{2}{21}$ c. chili
$\frac{1}{3}$ × $\frac{2}{9}$ = $\frac{2}{27}$ c. garlic

2.
$\frac{1}{2}$ × $\frac{1}{4}$ = $\frac{1}{8}$ c. Tabasco
$\frac{1}{2}$ × $\frac{1}{3}$ = $\frac{1}{6}$ c. red onions
$\frac{1}{2}$ × $\frac{2}{5}$ = $\frac{1}{5}$ c. horseradish
$\frac{1}{2}$ × $\frac{1}{6}$ = $\frac{1}{12}$ c. cayenne
$\frac{1}{2}$ × $\frac{3}{8}$ = $\frac{3}{16}$ c. mustard
$\frac{1}{2}$ × $\frac{2}{7}$ = $\frac{1}{7}$ c. chili
$\frac{1}{2}$ × $\frac{2}{9}$ = $\frac{1}{9}$ c. garlic

3.
$\frac{5}{6}$ × $\frac{1}{4}$ = $\frac{5}{24}$ c. Tabasco
$\frac{5}{6}$ × $\frac{1}{3}$ = $\frac{5}{18}$ c. red onions
$\frac{5}{6}$ × $\frac{2}{5}$ = $\frac{1}{3}$ c. horseradish
$\frac{5}{6}$ × $\frac{1}{6}$ = $\frac{5}{36}$ c. cayenne
$\frac{5}{6}$ × $\frac{3}{8}$ = $\frac{5}{16}$ c. mustard
$\frac{5}{6}$ × $\frac{2}{7}$ = $\frac{5}{21}$ c. chili
$\frac{5}{6}$ × $\frac{2}{9}$ = $\frac{5}{27}$ c. garlic

4.
$\frac{1}{4}$ × $\frac{1}{4}$ = $\frac{1}{16}$ c. Tabasco
$\frac{1}{4}$ × $\frac{1}{3}$ = $\frac{1}{12}$ c. red onions
$\frac{1}{4}$ × $\frac{2}{5}$ = $\frac{1}{10}$ c. horseradish
$\frac{1}{4}$ × $\frac{1}{6}$ = $\frac{1}{24}$ c. cayenne
$\frac{1}{4}$ × $\frac{3}{8}$ = $\frac{3}{32}$ c. mustard
$\frac{1}{4}$ × $\frac{2}{7}$ = $\frac{1}{14}$ c. chili
$\frac{1}{4}$ × $\frac{2}{9}$ = $\frac{1}{18}$ c. garlic

Page 84

Eartha Wurm's New Pizzas

Name _____

Eartha Wurm believes that pizzas have become flat, dull, tasteless and boring. She has created new pizza toppings to put some zing back into your taste buds.

Work the problems on another paper.   Answer Space

1. $7 \div \frac{1}{5} = 7 \times \frac{5}{1} = 35$

2. $15 \div \frac{1}{6} = 15 \times \frac{6}{1} = 90$

3. $12 \div \frac{2}{7} = {}^{6}\cancel{12} \times \frac{7}{2} = 42$

4. $10 \div \frac{1}{4} = 10 \times \frac{4}{1} = 40$

5. $40 \div \frac{1}{3} = 40 \times \frac{3}{1} = 120$

6. $16 \div \frac{2}{9} = {}^{8}\cancel{16} \times \frac{9}{2} = 72$

7. $6 \div \frac{3}{7} = {}^{2}\cancel{6} \times \frac{7}{3} = 14$

8. $18 \div \frac{3}{5} = {}^{6}\cancel{18} \times \frac{5}{3} = 30$

9. $4 \div \frac{4}{9} = \cancel{4} \times \frac{9}{4} = 9$

10. $20 \div \frac{5}{12} = {}^{4}\cancel{20} \times \frac{12}{5} = 48$

Answer Key

Kookey's Cubic Cookie Cakes

Professor Kook E. Kookey, inventor of the cubic cookie, has now created the ultimate dessert, the cubic cookie cake, loaded with sweet things to make your taste buds tingle.

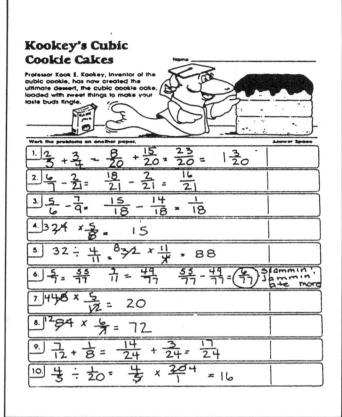

Work the problems on another paper.

Answer Space

1. $\frac{2}{5} + \frac{3}{4} = \frac{8}{20} + \frac{15}{20} = \frac{23}{20} = 1\frac{3}{20}$

2. $\frac{6}{7} - \frac{2}{21} = \frac{18}{21} - \frac{2}{21} = \frac{16}{21}$

3. $\frac{5}{6} - \frac{7}{9} = \frac{15}{18} - \frac{14}{18} = \frac{1}{18}$

4. $3\cancel{24} \times \frac{5}{8} = 15$

5. $32 \div \frac{4}{11} = \cancel{32}^8 \times \frac{11}{\cancel{4}} = 88$

6. $\frac{5}{7} = \frac{55}{77} \quad \frac{7}{11} = \frac{49}{77} \quad \frac{55}{77} - \frac{49}{77} = \left(\frac{6}{77}\right)$ Slammin' Jammin' ate more

7. $\cancel{48}^4 \times \frac{5}{\cancel{12}} = 20$

8. $\cancel{84}^{12} \times \frac{6}{\cancel{7}} = 72$

9. $\frac{7}{12} + \frac{1}{8} = \frac{14}{24} + \frac{3}{24} = \frac{17}{24}$

10. $\frac{4}{5} \div \frac{1}{20} = \frac{4}{5} \times \frac{\cancel{20}^4}{1} = 16$

Page 85

Mr. M.T. Whole's Doughnut Shoppe

Mr. M.T. Whole bakes doughnuts that make your whole body quiver with anticipation. He's especially proud of his Jam-Crammed Jelly Doughnuts and his Creamy Delights.

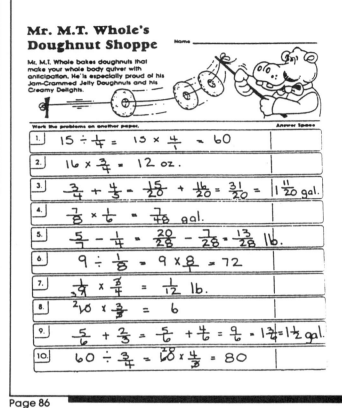

Work the problems on another paper.

Answer Space

1. $15 \div \frac{1}{4} = 15 \times \frac{4}{1} = 60$

2. $16 \times \frac{3}{4} = 12$ oz.

3. $\frac{3}{4} + \frac{4}{5} = \frac{15}{20} + \frac{16}{20} = \frac{31}{20} = 1\frac{11}{20}$ gal.

4. $\frac{7}{8} \times \frac{1}{6} = \frac{7}{48}$ gal.

5. $\frac{5}{7} - \frac{1}{4} = \frac{20}{28} - \frac{7}{28} = \frac{13}{28}$ lb.

6. $9 \div \frac{1}{8} = 9 \times \frac{8}{1} = 72$

7. $\frac{1}{3\cancel{9}} \times \frac{3}{4} = \frac{1}{12}$ lb.

8. $\cancel{10}^2 \times \frac{3}{5} = 6$

9. $\frac{5}{6} + \frac{2}{3} = \frac{5}{6} + \frac{4}{6} = \frac{9}{6} = 1\frac{3}{6} = 1\frac{1}{2}$ gal.

10. $60 \div \frac{3}{4} = \cancel{60}^{20} \times \frac{4}{\cancel{3}} = 80$

Page 86

Mean Monster Meets Molly Mugwumps

It was love at first bite. They met at Sam Sillicook's Pizza Palace, and neither person had a dainty appetite. Figure out how much they ate.

Work the problems on another paper.

Answer Space

1. $2\frac{1}{3} + 1\frac{1}{2} = \frac{7}{3} + \frac{13}{12} = \frac{28}{12} + \frac{13}{12} = \frac{41}{12}$ | $3\frac{5}{12}$

2. $10\frac{7}{8} - 3\frac{1}{2} = \frac{87}{8} - \frac{7}{2} = \frac{87}{8} - \frac{28}{8} = \frac{59}{8}$ | $7\frac{3}{8}$

3. $2\frac{5}{6} - 1\frac{1}{3} = \frac{17}{6} - \frac{4}{3} = \frac{17}{6} - \frac{8}{6} = \frac{9}{6} = 1\frac{3}{6}$ | $1\frac{1}{2}$

4. $5\frac{1}{2} + 4\frac{1}{3} = \frac{11}{2} + \frac{13}{3} = \frac{33}{6} + \frac{26}{6} = \frac{59}{6}$ | $9\frac{5}{6}$

5. $6\frac{7}{10} - 3\frac{2}{5} = \frac{67}{10} - \frac{17}{5} = \frac{67}{10} - \frac{34}{10} = \frac{33}{10}$ | $3\frac{3}{10}$

6. $6\frac{7}{8} - 5\frac{3}{4} = \frac{55}{8} - \frac{23}{4} = \frac{55}{8} - \frac{46}{8} = \frac{9}{8}$ | $1\frac{1}{8}$

7. $4\frac{1}{3} - 2\frac{1}{5} = \frac{13}{3} - \frac{11}{5} = \frac{65}{15} - \frac{33}{15} = \frac{32}{15}$ | $2\frac{2}{15}$

8. $6\frac{5}{8} - 2\frac{1}{2} = \frac{53}{8} - \frac{5}{2} = \frac{53}{8} - \frac{20}{8} = \frac{33}{8}$ | $4\frac{1}{8}$ lbs.

9. $5\frac{9}{10} - 2\frac{1}{4} = \frac{59}{10} - \frac{9}{4} = \frac{118}{20} - \frac{45}{20} = \frac{73}{20}$ | $3\frac{13}{20}$

10. $2\frac{3}{5} + 3\frac{1}{10} = \frac{13}{5} + \frac{31}{10} = \frac{26}{10} + \frac{31}{10} = \frac{57}{10}$ | $5\frac{7}{10}$

Page 87

Smelly Belly's Perfume Parlor

Smelly Belly is a skunk with a very refined sense of smell. She has started her own perfume business so that others can have an opportunity to enjoy all of her fragrances. Some of her favorite perfumes are Stinkpot, Stench and Fusty Musty.

Work the problems on another paper.

Answer Space

1. $3\frac{1}{3} \times 2\frac{1}{4} = \frac{\cancel{10}^5}{3} \times \frac{9^3}{\cancel{4}_2} = \frac{15}{2} = 7\frac{1}{2}$ gal.

2. $8\frac{1}{3} \times 2\frac{2}{5} = \frac{5\cancel{25}}{\cancel{3}} \times \frac{\cancel{12}^4}{\cancel{5}} = 20$ gal.

3. $5\frac{1}{4} \times 3\frac{3}{7} = \frac{3\cancel{21}}{\cancel{4}_1} \times \frac{\cancel{24}^6}{\cancel{7}} = 18$ cases

4. $6 \times 4\frac{1}{3} = \frac{\cancel{6}^2}{1} \times \frac{13}{\cancel{3}_1} = 26$ oz.

5. $20 \times 1\frac{1}{2} = \frac{\cancel{20}^{10}}{1} \times \frac{3}{\cancel{2}} = 30$ oz.

6. $7\frac{1}{3} \times \frac{9}{11} = \frac{2\cancel{22}}{\cancel{3}_1} \times \frac{9^3}{\cancel{11}} = 6$ cases

7. $18 \times 2\frac{1}{9} = \frac{\cancel{18}^2}{1} \times \frac{19}{\cancel{9}_1} = 38$ oz.

8. $7\frac{1}{2} \times 3\frac{3}{5} = \frac{3\cancel{15}}{2} \times \frac{18^9}{\cancel{5}} = 27$ cases

9. $2\frac{5}{6} \times 1\frac{1}{5} = \frac{17}{\cancel{6}} \times \frac{\cancel{6}^1}{5} = \frac{17}{5} = 3\frac{2}{5}$ oz.

10. $7\frac{1}{5} \times 2\frac{2}{9} = \frac{4\cancel{36}}{\cancel{5}} \times \frac{\cancel{20}^4}{\cancel{9}_1} = 16$ oz.

Page 88

Answer Key

Krab E. Krabby

Krab E. Krabby likes to make unusual things, but he gets very cranky trying to figure out how much material he needs. Give him a hand so he won't be crabby.

Name _____

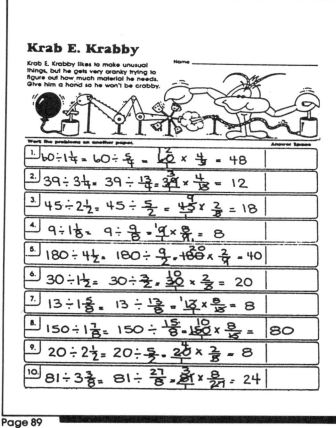

Work the problems on another paper.

Answer Space

1. $60 \div 1\frac{1}{4} = 60 \div \frac{5}{4} = \frac{12}{60} \times \frac{4}{5} = 48$

2. $39 \div 3\frac{1}{4} = 39 \div \frac{13}{4} = \frac{3}{39} \times \frac{4}{13} = 12$

3. $45 \div 2\frac{1}{2} = 45 \div \frac{5}{2} = \frac{9}{45} \times \frac{2}{5} = 18$

4. $9 \div 1\frac{1}{8} = 9 \div \frac{9}{8} = \frac{1}{9} \times \frac{8}{9} = 8$

5. $180 \div 4\frac{1}{2} = 180 \div \frac{9}{2} = \frac{20}{180} \times \frac{2}{9} = 40$

6. $30 \div 1\frac{1}{2} = 30 \div \frac{3}{2} = \frac{10}{30} \times \frac{2}{3} = 20$

7. $13 \div 1\frac{5}{8} = 13 \div \frac{13}{8} = \frac{1}{13} \times \frac{8}{13} = 8$

8. $150 \div 1\frac{7}{8} = 150 \div \frac{15}{8} = \frac{10}{150} \times \frac{8}{15} = $ 80

9. $20 \div 2\frac{1}{2} = 20 \div \frac{5}{2} = \frac{4}{20} \times \frac{2}{5} = 8$

10. $81 \div 3\frac{3}{8} = 81 \div \frac{27}{8} = \frac{3}{81} \times \frac{8}{27} = 24$

Page 89

Mr. M.T. Whole Creates the Super Twist

Mr. M.T. Whole has invented a whole new kind of doughnut which he calls the Super Twist. It is filled with whipped cream, jammed with jelly and topped with powdered sugar.

Name _____

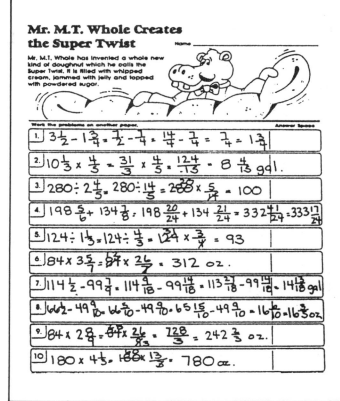

Work the problems on another paper.

Answer Space

1. $3\frac{1}{2} - 1\frac{3}{4} = \frac{7}{2} - \frac{7}{4} = \frac{14}{4} - \frac{7}{4} = \frac{7}{4} = 1\frac{3}{4}$

2. $10\frac{1}{3} \times \frac{4}{5} = \frac{31}{3} \times \frac{4}{5} = \frac{124}{15} = 8\frac{4}{15}$ gal.

3. $280 \div 2\frac{4}{5} = 280 \div \frac{14}{5} = \frac{20}{280} \times \frac{5}{14} = 100$

4. $198\frac{5}{6} + 134\frac{7}{8} = 198\frac{20}{24} + 134\frac{21}{24} = 332\frac{41}{24} = 333\frac{17}{24}$

5. $124 \div 1\frac{1}{3} = 124 \div \frac{4}{3} = \frac{31}{124} \times \frac{3}{4} = 93$

6. $84 \times 3\frac{5}{7} = \frac{12}{84} \times \frac{26}{7} = 312$ oz.

7. $114\frac{1}{2} - 99\frac{7}{9} = 114\frac{9}{18} - 99\frac{14}{18} = 113\frac{27}{18} - 99\frac{14}{18} = 14\frac{13}{18}$ gal.

8. $66\frac{1}{2} - 49\frac{9}{10} = 66\frac{5}{10} - 49\frac{9}{10} = 65\frac{15}{10} - 49\frac{9}{10} = 16\frac{6}{10} = 16\frac{3}{5}$ oz.

9. $84 \times 2\frac{8}{9} = \frac{28}{84} \times \frac{26}{9} = \frac{728}{3} = 242\frac{2}{3}$ oz.

10. $180 \times 4\frac{1}{3} = \frac{60}{180} \times \frac{13}{3} = 780$ oz.

Page 90

McMealworms Introduce the Super Sac

McMealworms wants your business. They have just introduced the Super Sac, a triple decker McMealworm Burger that comes with Roasted Roaches and a Cricket Cola.

Name _____

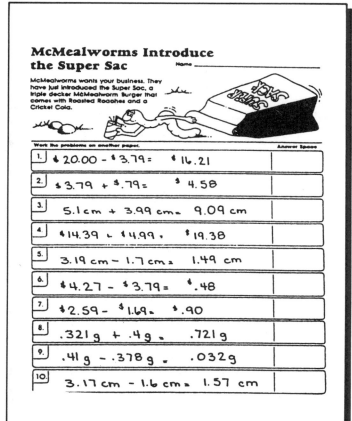

Work the problems on another paper.

Answer Space

1. $\$20.00 - \$3.79 = \$16.21$

2. $\$3.79 + \$.79 = \$4.58$

3. $5.1\,cm + 3.99\,cm = 9.09\,cm$

4. $\$14.39 + \$4.99 = \$19.38$

5. $3.19\,cm - 1.7\,cm = 1.49\,cm$

6. $\$4.27 - \$3.79 = \$.48$

7. $\$2.59 - \$1.69 = \$.90$

8. $.321\,g + .4\,g = .721\,g$

9. $.41\,g - .378\,g = .032\,g$

10. $3.17\,cm - 1.6\,cm = 1.57\,cm$

Page 91

Kookey's Cubic Cookie Candy Bar

Professor Kook E. Kookey has invented a cookie that is shaped like a child's alphabet block and tastes like a super sweet candy bar. He also has cubic cookie candy bars that are crammed with berries and chunks of chocolate.

Name _____

Work the problems on another paper.

Answer Space

1. $35 \times 3.7 = 129.5$ oz.

2. $68 \times 5.3 = 360.4$ oz.

3. $6.78 \times .25 = 1.695$ oz.

4. $5.34 \times .25 = 1.335$ oz.

5. $12.306 \times 3.5 = 43.071$ oz.

6. $30.5 \times 7.5 = 228.75$ oz.

7. $40 \times 11.504 = 460.16$ oz.

8. $4.67 \times .33 = 1.5411$ oz.

9. $200 \times 5.6 = 1120$ oz.

10. $28 \times 2.013 = 56.364$ oz.

Page 92

Answer Key

You and Major League Baseball

You have won a national contest sponsored by Oleg's Groaty Oaties. The prize is a chance for you to play in the majors. All you have to do is bat over .300 against the majority of the major leaguers. **Reminder:** To find your batting averages divide the number of "at bats" into the number of "hits." Add a decimal point and 3 zeroes to the number of hits.

Work the problems on another paper.

		Answer Space
1.	$4 \div 10 =$ .400	
2.	$16 \div 20 =$ .800	
3.	$7 \div 14 =$ .500	
4.	$13 \div 20 =$ .650	
5.	$9 \div 12 =$ .750	
6.	$5 \div 8 =$ .625	
7.	$2 \div 10 =$ .200	
8.	$12 \div 16 =$ .750	
9.	$17 \div 20 =$ .850	
10.	$114 \div 175 =$ .651	

Page 93

Creepy Crawly Critters

Work the problems on another paper.

		Answer Space
1.	.9 mm x 250 = 2250 mm	
2.	2.5 cm + 3.499 cm = 5.999 cm	
3.	20 cm x 4.1 = 82 cm	
4.	134.6 cm - 60.9 cm = 73.7 cm	
5.	5.84 m - 4.6 m = 1.24 m	
6.	106.699 cm - 42.8 cm = 63.899 cm	
7.	1.5 cm x 1.334 = 2.001 cm	
8.	1.3 cm x 1.611 = 2.0943 cm	
9.	157.50 cm ÷ 225 = .7 cm	
10.	1856 cm ÷ 32 = 5.8 cm	

Page 94

The N.B.A. Wants You

You have just been named "The Young Basketball Player of the Year." Your reward is a chance to go one-on-one against the superstars of the N.B.A.

Instructions: Compute your shooting percentage and round it off to the nearest whole percent.

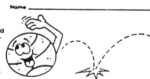

Work the problems on another paper.

		Answer Space
1.	$13 \div 20 =$ 65%	
2.	$3 \div 20 =$ 15%	
3.	$15 \div 25 =$ 60%	
4.	$8 \div 25 =$ 32%	
5.	$7 \div 14 =$ 50%	
6.	$6 \div 14 =$ 43%	
7.	$9 \div 12 =$ 75%	
8.	$2 \div 12 =$ 17%	
9.	$15 \div 22 =$ 68%	
10.	$4 \div 22 =$ 18%	

Page 95

The National Football League Wants You!

You were so spectacular in your last school football game that every team in the N.F.L. wanted to draft you as their number 1 quarterback. You ended up with a new team that really needed your help, the Old Dold Outlaws.

Compute your passing percentage against these teams to the nearest whole percent.

Work the problems on another paper.

		Answer Space
1.	$25 \div 30 =$ 83%	
2.	$16 \div 24 =$ 67%	
3.	$11 \div 16 =$ 69%	
4.	$17 \div 25 =$ 68%	
5.	$33 \div 36 =$ 92%	
6.	$28 \div 40 =$ 70%	
7.	$11 \div 34 =$ 32%	
8.	$37 \div 42 =$ 88%	
9.	$7 \div 23 =$ 30%	
10.	$234 \div 298 =$ 79%	

Page 96

Answer Key

Time Out for Molly Mugwumps

Molly Mugwumps is disorganized. Her room looks like it was designed by a hurricane, her closet is stuffed full of stuff, and her locker is a disaster. She especially needs help managing her time.

Work the problems on another paper.   Answer Space

1.	7:17 a.m.	
2.	8:21 a.m.	
3.	40 minutes	
4.	11:33 a.m.	
5.	4:23 p.m.	
6.	6:02 p.m.	
7.	2:44 p.m.	
8.	9:06 p.m.	
9.	6:48 a.m.	
10.	4 hours 47 min.	

Page 97

Mean Monster Puts a Lock on Wrestling

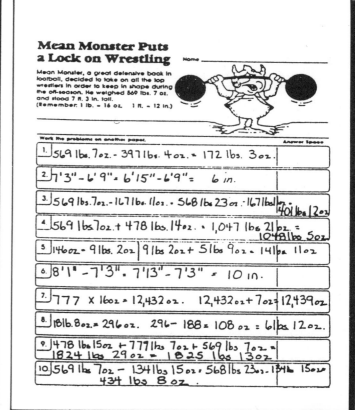

Mean Monster, a great defensive back in football, decided to take on all the top wrestlers in order to keep in shape during the off-season. He weighed 869 lbs. 7 oz. and stood 7 ft. 3 in. tall.
(Remember: 1 lb. = 16 oz.   1 ft. = 12 in.)

Work the problems on another paper.   Answer Space

1.	569 lbs. 7 oz. - 397 lbs. 4 oz. = 172 lbs. 3 oz.	
2.	7'3" - 6'9" = 6'15" - 6'9" = 6 in.	
3.	569 lbs. 7 oz. - 167 lbs. 11 oz. = 568 lbs 23 oz - 167 lbs 11 oz = 401 lbs 12 oz	
4.	569 lbs 7 oz + 478 lbs. 14 oz. = 1,047 lbs 21 oz = 1048 lbs 5 oz	
5.	146 oz = 9 lbs. 2 oz 9 lbs 2 oz + 5 lbs 9 oz = 14 lbs 11 oz	
6.	8'1" - 7'3" = 7'13" - 7'3" = 10 in.	
7.	777 x 16 oz = 12,432 oz. 12,432 oz + 7 oz = 12,439 oz	
8.	18 lb. 8 oz = 296 oz. 296 - 188 = 108 oz = 6 lbs 12 oz.	
9.	478 lbs 15 oz + 777 lbs 7 oz + 569 lbs 7 oz = 1824 lbs 29 oz = 1825 lbs 13 oz	
10.	569 lbs 7 oz - 134 lbs 15 oz = 568 lbs 23 oz - 134 lbs 15 oz = 434 lbs 8 oz .	

Page 98

Molly Cleans up the School . . . Sort Of

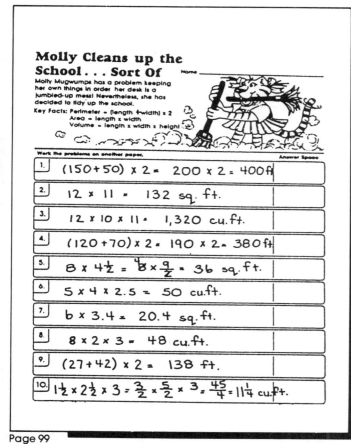

Molly Mugwumps has a problem keeping her own things in order, her desk is a jumbled-up mess! Nevertheless, she has decided to tidy up the school.

Key Facts: Perimeter = (length + width) x 2
Area = length x width
Volume = length x width x height

Work the problems on another paper.   Answer Space

1.	(150 + 50) x 2 = 200 x 2 = 400 ft	
2.	12 x 11 = 132 sq. ft.	
3.	12 x 10 x 11 = 1,320 cu. ft.	
4.	(120 + 70) x 2 = 190 x 2 = 380 ft	
5.	$8 \times 4\frac{1}{2} = 8 \times \frac{9}{2} = 36$ sq. ft.	
6.	5 x 4 x 2.5 = 50 cu. ft.	
7.	6 x 3.4 = 20.4 sq. ft.	
8.	8 x 2 x 3 = 48 cu. ft.	
9.	(27 + 42) x 2 = 138 ft.	
10.	$1\frac{1}{2} \times 2\frac{1}{2} \times 3 = \frac{3}{2} \times \frac{5}{2} \times 3 = \frac{45}{4} = 11\frac{1}{4}$ cu. ft.	

Page 99

It's for the Birds

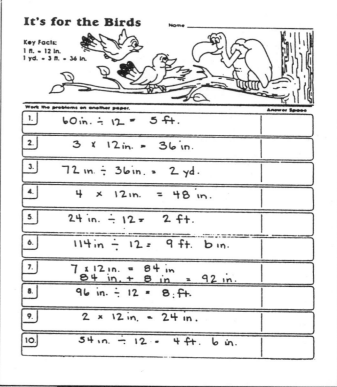

Key Facts:
1 ft. = 12 in.
1 yd. = 3 ft. = 36 in.

Work the problems on another paper.   Answer Space

1.	60 in. ÷ 12 = 5 ft.	
2.	3 x 12 in. = 36 in.	
3.	72 in. ÷ 36 in. = 2 yd.	
4.	4 x 12 in. = 48 in.	
5.	24 in. ÷ 12 = 2 ft.	
6.	114 in. ÷ 12 = 9 ft. 6 in.	
7.	7 x 12 in. = 84 in 84 in. + 8 in. = 92 in.	
8.	96 in. ÷ 12 = 8 ft.	
9.	2 x 12 in. = 24 in.	
10.	54 in. ÷ 12 = 4 ft. 6 in.	

Page 100

127   IF8747 Math Topics

Answer Key

Metric Measurement: The Bear Facts

Name _____

Key Facts:
1 meter = 100 centimeters = 1000 millimeters
1 centimeter = 10 millimeters

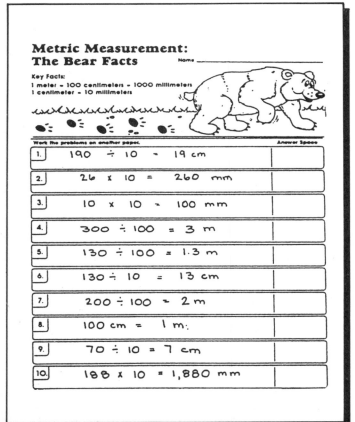

Work the problems on another paper.   Answer Space

1.	190 ÷ 10 = 19 cm
2.	26 x 10 = 260 mm
3.	10 x 10 = 100 mm
4.	300 ÷ 100 = 3 m
5.	130 ÷ 100 = 1.3 m
6.	130 ÷ 10 = 13 cm
7.	200 ÷ 100 = 2 m
8.	100 cm = 1 m
9.	70 ÷ 10 = 7 cm
10.	188 x 10 = 1,880 mm

Page 101

Leapin' Lizards

Name _____

Key Facts:
1 meter = 100 centimeters = 1000 millimeters
10 millimeters = 1 centimeter

Work the problems on another paper.   Answer Space

1.	40.6 x 10 = 406 mm
2.	61 ÷ 100 = .61 m
3.	63.5 - 30.6 = 32.9 cm
4.	100 - 26.7 = 73.3 cm
5.	100 - 40.6 = 59.4 cm
6.	25 + 13.7 = 38.7 cm
7.	200 - 38.4 = 161.6 cm
8.	200 ÷ 100 = 2 m
9.	35.6 x 10 = 356 mm
10.	26.6 - 14.9 = 11.7 cm

Page 102

About the book . . .

This book contains activity pages on such math topics as time, money, measurement and graphing, plus story problems with humorous twists and logical approaches to help students solve each one.

Credits . . .
Authors: Jan Kennedy, James E. Davidson, Ph.D., Robert W. Smith, Bill Linderman
Editors: Jackie Servis, Rhonda DeWaard and Mina McMullin
Artists: Karen Caminata, Jim Price, Carol Tiernon, Jeffrey Liem
Production: Ann Dyer and Kurt Kemperman
Cover Photo: Dan Van Duinen